MATERIAL MAN

MASCULINITY SEXUALITY STYLE

PITTI
IMMAGINE   fashion
engineering

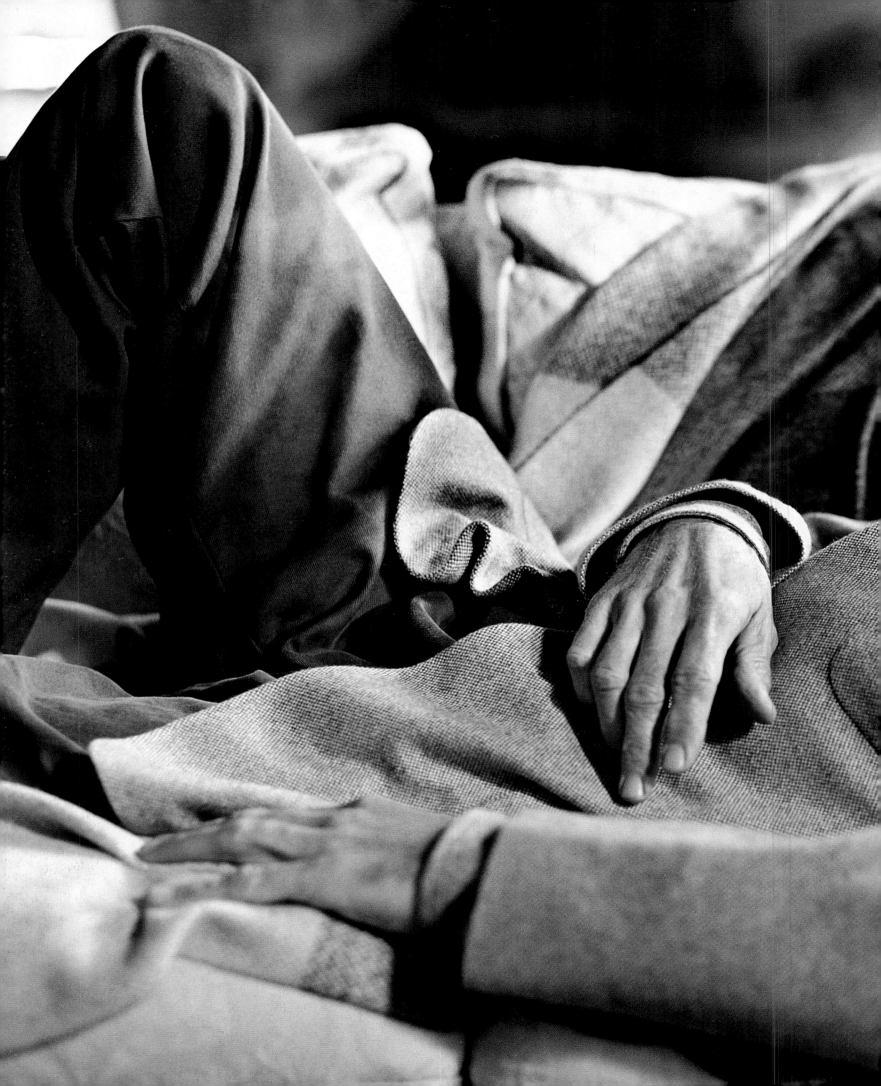

preceding pages:

Carnival in
Sciacca, Sicily.
Photo by Franco
Zecchin

Picture from the
1998 advertising
campaign *Home
Sweet Home
Welcome to
Marlboro Country*

Fitness fair,
Rimini 1995.
Photo by Armin
Linke

Kookaï,
spring/summer
1999 advertising
campaign

Fiorucci
1974 advertising
campaign

Gianfranco Ferré,
spring/summer
1997 jeans
collection.
Photo by
Domenico Stinellis

Ermenegildo
Zegna, fall/winter
1998/99.
Photo by Mikael
Jansson

MATERIAL MAN

MASCULINITY SEXUALITY STYLE

Edited by
Giannino Malossi

Harry N. Abrams, Inc., Publishers

Curator
Giannino Malossi

Exhibition Design
Pierluigi Cerri

Special Consultants
Carlo Bertelli
Peppino Ortoleva

Photo Editing
Giannino Malossi

*Assistant to the Editor
and Curator
Image Research*
Antonella Mazza

Research
Cinzia Minola/Cult Media Ltd.

Press Office
Cristina Brigidini

Public Relations
Sibilla della Gherardesca

Administrative Supervisor
Sybille Bollmann

Exhibition Supervisor
Anna Pazzagli

Video
Show Biz
Ranuccio Sodi, Romano Frassa,
Carmelo Marabello,
Gaetano Vaudo

*Sound track of the exhibition
conceived and produced by*
RAI RADIO TRE

*Editorial Coordinator
and Book Packager*
Progetto Media, Milan

Graphic Design
Barbara Capanni

Publishing Consultant
Antony Shugaar

English-language Editor
Eric Himmel

Editorial Coordinator, USA
Paraculture, NY

Translations
Guido Lagomarsino
Antony Shugaar

Image Research
Antonella Mazza

Production Director
Carla Mantero—Progetto Media

Special Printing Consultant
Antonio Maffeis

**FASHION
ENGINEERING
UNIT™**

Material Man
Masculinity Sexuality Style

Florence, Stazione Leopolda
January 14-30, 2000

Pitti Immagine, srl

Mario Boselli
President

Raffaello Napoleone
*General Manager
and Managing Director*

Lapo Cianchi
*Director of Corporate
Communications
and Special Projects*

Giannino Malossi
*Director of the Fashion
Engineering Unit*

FASHION
ENGINEERING
UNIT™®

Previous publications

The Style Engine, 1998

*Volare: The Icon of Italy in
Global Pop Culture*, 1999

Library of Congress Catalog Card
Number: 99-67946
ISBN 0-8109-2709-8

Copyright © 2000 Pitti Immagine

Published in 2000
by Harry N. Abrams, Incorporated,
New York
Harry N. Abrams, Inc., NY
Printed and bound in Italy
Poligrafiche Bolis, Bergamo

Harry N. Abrams, Inc.
100 Fifth Avenue
New York, N.Y. 10011
www.abramsbooks.com

CONTENTS

this page: Gucci,
fall/winter
1998/99 collection

preceding page:
Prada, fall/winter
1995/96
advertising
campaign with
John Malkovich.
Photo by
Peter Lindberg

overleaf:
Laura Biagiotti,
spring/summer
2000 menswear
collection. Photo
by Luca Bruno

Material Man is the third research project undertaken by the Fashion Engineering Unit, Pitti Immagine's think tank, devoted to providing cultural analysis of fashion and the textiles/apparel industry. With the foundation of the Fashion Engineering Unit, Pitti Immagine inaugurated a unique structure meant to provide a systematic analysis of the creation of added value through the coordinated processes of design, communications, and style (in a word, product innovation), features that distinguish work being done in the fashion field today.

In 1998 the Fashion Engineering Unit produced the book and exhibition *The Style Engine*, an exploration of the forms of creative intelligence that fashion contributes to the fields of entertainment, design, business, and the production of individual and social identity; in 1999 the program continued with *Volare: The Icon of Italy in Global Pop Culture*, which focused on "Italian style" and the way that various industries, including the fashion industry, manage to include features of everyday Italian culture in goods that are meant to circulate in the world's markets. This third project is devoted to the contemporary image of masculinity, analyzed largely in the context of men's fashion.

Fashion, which emphasizes the present while conceiving of it as the future, offers a perspective that has been widely overlooked in the general discourse on design and culture, increasingly a central topic of mass culture. Thanks to the contributions from the scholars and experts that the Fashion Engineering Unit has assembled, a new view is emerging of the complex nature of production and communication in the fashion industry, resulting perhaps in a slightly better and deeper understanding of what fashion is and how it operates. They present a clearer picture of fashion as a crossroads of varied interests, a genuine global industry, and a vast workshop that requires intense participation in the culture of its time in order to develop and grow. This is precisely the focus of the work that Pitti Immagine has done over the past few years, developing an original body of work in the international panorama of fashion shows and trade fairs.

I hope that once again this new project may prove useful to experts and those working in the field of fashion, and for anyone who is interested in fashion; without a doubt, it has been useful to those of us at Pitti Immagine who are working to create greater opportunities and wider horizons for this remarkable undertaking.

Mario Boselli
President of Pitti Immagine

Every six months, following the presentation of the new collections, men's fashion designers sit down with others in the industry and think long and hard about the identity and the future of man. The attention of one and all is usually focused on the most remarkable stylistic innovations and the most daring new products to emerge in the recent past, while the insights and ideas—often subtle and perceptive—hidden in those innovations and products generally remain in the shadows: fashion creativity is thus inevitably downgraded to mere flair; its ideas become little more than publicity stunts. *Material Man* is an attempt to understand the mechanisms that influence the identity and the future of man more clearly. It eschews the short term and the evanescent in an effort to delve into more concrete, longer-term factors by calling upon the work of scholars of the social sciences, scholars who have been asking many of the same questions for many years, but in isolation from each other.

I cannot say with any certainty just when the explosive crisis in masculine identity began, but I can certainly say that the modern fashion industry would seem to have benefited from it considerably, since for a number of years now worldwide volume of consumption of men's apparel and accessories has been roughly equal to the consumption of women's apparel and accessories. Certainly, the crisis has led to an exponential increase in the variety of offerings and freedom of choice in the field of men's fashion: the construction of an identity has become more complex and personal, less regulated by external social forces. For the fashion industry these changes have demanded a growing attention to the dynamics of consumption as opposed to the dynamics of production. This has made for a more challenging field, but a field that is increasingly open to any and all competitors.

It is not happenstance that an undertaking like *Material Man* should have been developed by Pitti Immagine's research wing: we at Pitti Immagine Uomo have always striven to understand the deeper background radiation emerging from the progressive fragmentation of the unified image of masculinity, attempting in our projects to reflect—and at times, foreshadow—the many facets and fluctuations of that image.

Raffaello Napoleone
General Manager and Managing Director of Pitti Immagine

Giannino Malossi

MATERIAL MAN

Decoding Fashion, Redefining Masculinity

The things you see these days. There's a man in the shower, naked, a great big man who could be a truck driver, a boxer, or a football player . . . An archetypal male, with a shaved head and determined gestures, radiating the confidence that comes from an unexamined relationship with one's gender.

He is covering his body with a soft, white bath foam, the big brute. The camera continues to focus on his massive biceps, his athletic torso. Already the foaming gel that slides down the skin and muscles of this tough guy produces a vaguely unsettling effect. . . . But when this latter-day Hercules, who is black by the way, realizes that he is being filmed, and addresses the audience, the real surprise hits: in a falsetto, a man imitating a woman's voice, the big guy explains his preference for the product, parodying the movements and demeanor of girls doing a detergent commercial.

Another scene. A hall is crowded and overheated, as is required on these occasions; a select audience has gathered to view the new collection of a designer who built her fortune on the strength of her scandalous creations. In her day, the designer worked with a band that built its reputation on shattering the Anglo-Saxon taboo against insulting the queen; she later contributed to the postmodern redefinition of fashion by reinventing the corset, crinolines, and other Victorian systems for constricting the body. The audience, therefore, awaits this season's new outrage. Nobody knows what it will be.

On the runway there appears, amidst general excitement, a man, wobbling and swaying on a pair of stiletto heels . . . but not a transvestite, that's old hat, ever since the evening news started carrying coverage of fashion shows. This is a real man. A man's man.

Scandal! Lots of coverage guaranteed in all the media the next day, which is one of the reasons for a fashion show. There is more. In the local section of a regional daily (and on the Internet!), but already poised to leap into the pages of a national newsweekly, there is a summer silly-season news story from Italy: the lifeguards of the Adriatic beachfront, renowned for their much acclaimed virility, are going to pose nude for a calendar. They will thus join a group of Milanese advertising executives and the entire population of a Ligurian resort town, who have posed nude for calendars of their own. . . . These are collateral effects, on a smaller scale, of the popularity of the film *The Full Monty* and the success of the Pirelli pinup calendar.

Gillian Wearing,
Signs..., 1992/93

Humphrey
Bogart in *Beat
the Devil*, 1953,
directed by John
Huston. Photo by
Robert Capa

facing page:
President Bill
Clinton, admitting
that he had an
"inappropriate"
relationship with
Monica Lewinsky:
"I misled people;
I deeply
regret that."
Washington, D.C.,
17 August 1998.
Photo by
Greg Gibson

These three minor events occurred over the course of the last few months in contemporary Western media territory, an undifferentiated space that ranges from American television all the way out to the Italian provinces. The commercial with a football fullback who makes fun of himself, a runway presentation with men— real men—teetering on high heels, and the calendar with lifeguards in their birthday suits offer an accurate representation of three degrees of the same theme.

What we are talking about is the way that masculinity and that which is masculine is typically conceived, depicted, and idealized today. We could, of course, mention a vast array of other signals that are zinging across the galaxy of global culture.

Fragments of the once solid construct of Western masculinity—or its image in terms of spectacle—are scattering on their own, spinning away in all directions.

The "crisis of the male" has become a cliché, a prefabricated topic ready to be trotted out in television debates, movies, and articles; the recent worldwide furor over Bill Clinton and Monica Lewinsky constitutes the most visible instance of the weakness of today's man within a context that has been exclusively favorable to male prerogatives: politics. The crossfire to which males are subjected these days—in the form of protests and questioning of gender identity and depiction of a general contemporary male perplexity and confusion—constitutes one of the most frequent and popular ploys of media communications and of fashion, which is, so to speak, the reified, objectified version of that communication transformed into tangible, salable products.

If, in reality, the crisis of the male is just a fashion, that doesn't mean that it is insignificant. Fashion, along with advertising and popular entertainment, are specific expressions of the surface layers of culture, but they deal with material that originates at a far deeper level. Fashions don't originate out of a clear blue sky. They move "in the direction that the wind is already blowing," as John C. Flugel wrote as early as 1930.

This doesn't mean we should assume that men of tomorrow will wear high heels (to the office, or to a football game?) because "we have reached this point" in a fashion runway presentation, but rather that the time we live in is beginning to question the rough shell that covers the male gender, a shell made up of gestures, poses, and states of mind that have "powerfully" characterized men in their external manifestations as much as in the way that men see themselves: i.e., a much more important change is under way.

Why is this happening? After all, the mask of "virile" masculinity has been a constant of the twentieth century, giving a face to the male domination that seems to be the natural state of things in the Western world.

Cracks in this wall began to appear shortly after the Second World War. Writing in Los Angeles in 1944, Theodore Adorno expressed an open mistrust of "the virile attitude, expressing independence, confidence in

the sense of command, and the tacit complicity of all males" in the "caprices of the ruler." A certain caution regarding the celebration of the one-dimensional male ought to have been suggested by the intrinsic affinities between images of virility and totalitarian regimes. The cult of the virile personality of the "chief" served to legitimate authoritarian governments, as was quite evident in the propaganda and popular culture organized by the cultural apparatuses of various authoritarian regimes when, in the twenty-year period from 1922 to 1942 (the period extending from the first establishment of Fascism to its greatest planetary expansion), "strong men" ruled 53 of the 65 existing sovereign states.

The man's man, however, was virtually unchallenged through the Fifties and Sixties. The decade of the Seventies promised the opportunity for a redefinition of genders; it was rejected. The return to normality in the Eighties concealed in the shadows the wrinkles and other signs of decline long evident on the "hard-boiled" physiognomy of masculinity.

Despite an interesting, and possibly suspect, correspondence between the new critique of masculinity and the recent uptick in consumption of cosmetics and makeup for men, there is no actual external threat to the male "ruling class," aside from the sheer inertia of its own unresolved internal contradictions. The subordinate status of women is still a universal state of affairs, here and there concealed behind a facade of political correctness. Suffice it to cite the statistics on female unemployment in Europe or women's wages in the United States: the picture is quite clear.

If we take a careful look at the actual distribution of power in government hierarchies and major corporations

all the way down to labor relations in the smallest and grittiest companies, we will quickly see that nothing has really changed. Moreover, the so-called crisis of the male is not matched by any crisis in the male esthetic canons that serve as the template—in feminine terms as well—for the ways in which society imagines, desires, and shapes women: think of "models" from Barbie to Claudia Schiffer or consider the invasion of female nudity into advertising, and we must agree that success is still smiling upon clichés that cannot be considered anything but old-style sexism.

Even though the male remains firmly in control, he implodes, collapsing due to internal fatigue, and as his image vanishes, all that remains is the empty shell of his desires. The man's man could be the real Y2K bug.

The reasons for the implosion of masculinity are numerous, going well beyond issues of gender specificity. In the essays that make up this book, several of them are explored: changes in the roles and conditions of life, and in the modes of production that affect men and women in diverse, though not different, ways.

But at least one reason for the general decline in the man's man is implicit in the internal dynamics of the communications and consumption of fashion, and in the economics of the spectacle that moderates relationships among people and between people and objects. A cynical and materialistic (and, therefore, masculine?) response to the question posed by the metamorphosis of the male can be formulated, beginning with considerations of the "immaterial" value of goods: the image of uniform, unnuanced virility is just not as profitable as is its opposite.

As we now know—and clothing offers just one of the more evident instances—goods contain economic value in their immaterial aspects, consisting of the cultural references that they express, the information and the signs that they incorporate. To offer just one example, a pair of jeans and a double-breasted suit are not actually very different, any more than a miniskirt and a woman's tailored outfit.

But they are different in terms of what Baudrillard calls "sign value." They create a different appearance, they modify the identity of the person who wears them. It is only a question of appearance, obviously, but in terms of appearance it is an important question.

After all, forms express the spirit of the time. As anyone walking around in the streets of present-day Florence (or Manhattan) dressed in leotard would soon experience directly, the sign value of clothes coincides with their function. This aspect of the substance of goods is highly valued in modern culture, and part of sign value is gender identity. It is precisely upon the possibility of expressing sign value, through design and

communications, that the fashion industry is focusing to create added value.

For that matter, the true function of commercial communications lies in the production of a shared view, a "common sense." The fashion and communications industries, by transforming the symbolic into economics, contribute to the creation, selection, and manipulation of new cultural images and facts, just as in botany, there is a constant quest for new hybrids and crossbreeds, better suited to specific purposes.

In the field of fashion, the primary requirement is to create goods and images that incorporate the greatest possible concentration of sign value and that are, for exactly this reason, easily replaceable and interchangeable. Nothing should be definitive and final in fashion. In order to allow all fashions to be the "very latest," the "last thing," none actually can be.

The mayor of New York City, Rudolph Giuliani, as a "transvestite" in a satirical revue

facing page: Anthony Quinn in *La Strada*, 1954, directed by Federico Fellini

Under the effect of fashion, the figure of the body, its movements, and its poses are continually being modified by the dynamic of signs.

Men's suits, which once lasted for a lifetime, corresponded to an idea of the body that remained unchanged. Suits and clothing that must change continually take for granted that the body is flexible and undetermined, along with the body's mental image.

The fashion industry has learned to control the flow of signs that generate this metamorphosis of the body.

The consumption of fashion, and the various forms of communication that accompany that consumption, tend in this context to become autonomous cultural expressions, freed from such external presuppositions as tradition and religious ideological conventions. From this point of view, the rigidity and the strict codification that were once characteristic of male identity, and which were "depicted" in men's fashion, have been outmoded, discarded to make way for the possibility of a far more nuanced, complex, and diversified range of variants on possible identities. This, in turn, translates into a far greater array of possible forms of consumption, that is, a greater circulation of goods. In other words, when a unified male identity was replaced by a manifold identity, wardrobes multiplied to match each of the possible new identities.

The motivation of the fashion industry and communications business, from this point of view, is quite evident: the more nuances of identity there are, the more possibilities there are for desire to be generated or stimulated, and the more suits, outfits, and accessories can be sold.

The vexed question of the length of men's hair, first posed successfully by the Beatles in the Sixties, the first planetary debut of the long-running road show, "Redefinition of Masculine Style," is another example. It seemed like a matter of crushing importance, the end of an eternal order in the conventions and confusion of the sexes, a metaphor of the disorders that were to ensue; it was actually a mere premise for a new universe of consumption that was advancing ineluctably.

Driven by the diversification triggered by the fashion business, the masculine shell is gradually becoming so thin that it is vanishing entirely, allowing a glimpse of something else whose final outline is not yet clearly defined, though the process itself is eminently evident.

If the image is separated from the thing it represents, it becomes autonomous, objective per se, and is easier to decipher, manipulate, and hijack for use in other forms and contexts. Even masculinity, the stereotypical archetype, has become, paradoxically, the outcome of a "project," a "design."

The problem is that it is precisely masculinity as such that is viewed as definitive, immanent, incorporating into its very nature rigidity that can withstand all events. A real man is a man of steel; a man with feet of clay is a metaphor for the negation of a real man. In the face of the expectation of immobility over time, the slightest appearance of change immediately becomes a threat and a shock. Humphrey Bogart, no longer young—at the time of *The African Queen*—was very concerned that the wrinkles of his face, the source of much of his charisma as a man with a past, might be canceled by the lights of the set, so that he might be made to seem like a "different" man, somehow less male.

If, however, the weight of the masculine world seems to press down on the male, we should also remember that the type of the "tough guy" male, who "scorns everything that doesn't reek of smoke, leather, and shaving cream" is not an absolute and immutable datum, but a cultural construct that coincided with the phase of the full and flourishing development of modernity. The type of the man's man, personified on a popular level in the faces of the actors of suspense, detective, and Western movies from the Thirties to the Fifties, flowed off of the silver screen into the alloy used to cast a visual image of masculinity that was manipulated by an organized system of production that, on the one hand, enormously increased the possibility of control over the economy, while on the other was widely experienced as a sharp reduction of the power of individuals over their own lives. On all of the faces of "tough guys" we can see, alongside the violence that will be unleashed with the next plot twist, a harshness imposed by the need to accept the stakes set by an external threat: a determined invader, a rival racket, a corrupt society. And it was by giving a face to the Everyman who was dealing with adaptation to modernity that photography and the movies burst onto the scene during the years between the two world wars.

Nowadays, the media game of which fashion is making use, the game of the spectacular scandal, derives from the enormous excitement generated by the reversal of the stereotype of male into a stereotype of crisis. It is the old trick employed to such good effect in the fable of the Emperor's New Clothes.

There is a fragment of powerful truth in every male image that does not correspond to the canons of male style, because each of these images allows us to glimpse another possibility, more or less improbable in reality but already visible in the world of the spectacle. The use that fashion makes of the male image constitutes the frontier where the image of the spectacle challenges common sense. Therefore, the question of the male image in fashion is, nowadays, the most interesting point of observation of the central role that fashion now plays in the everyday life of postindustrial societies.

Reference to the crisis of males and masculinity operates as a background metaphor for the countless discourses, vignettes, and references that constitute the narrative of the present day in the everyday spectacle. There, for example, there is always a perplexed, muddled male behind, and mirroring, every "successful" woman.

Again, the "successful" woman is just as much an imaginary construction of commercial culture. Or, for another example, in the worldwide advertising spot, once a secondary theater for the deeds of the man's man, we now increasingly see *"ominicchi,"* to use a term coined by the late Italian author, Leonardo Sciascia: pathetic little men, dazed, turned to jelly in the face of a perfect woman; at least, perfect in terms of compatibility with the imaginary world of merchandise.

Both of these dialectical situations juxtaposing a man and a woman, in any case, happily find a new equilibrium, a resolution, in a shared faith in new models of consumption. The troubled picture of gender confusion and the relations between the sexes is calmed and brightened, according to the metaphors of fashion, by a new automobile, a new electric appliance, or a new set of clothing.

Vivienne Westwood fall/winter 1998/99 collection. Photo by Antonio Calanni

facing page: Primo Carnera, world heavyweight boxing champion, taking golf lessons in Miami, 1934

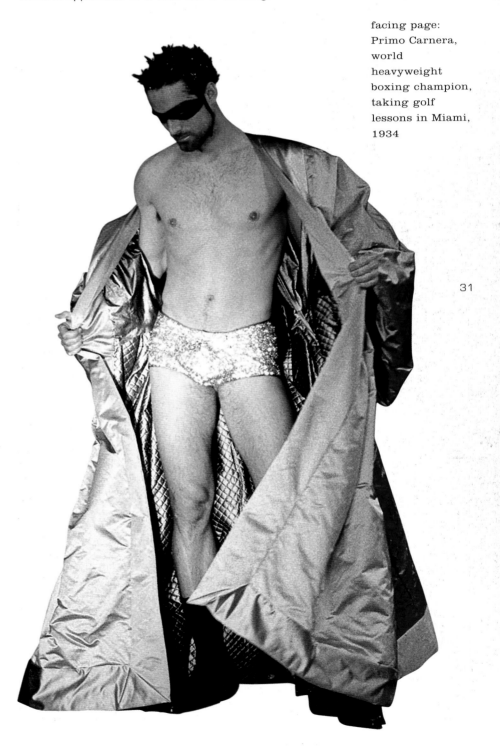

The Beatles with their makeup artists. Photo by David Hurn

A world of qualities without a man has arisen, of experiences without the person who experiences them, and it almost looks as though ideally private experience is a thing of the past, and that the friendly burden of personal responsibility is to dissolve into a system of formulas of possible meanings.

—Robert Musil, *The Man Without Qualities*

Franco La Cecla

ROUGH MANNERS

How Men Are Made

To speak of masculinity in general, sui generis, must be avoided at all costs. It is as a discourse of self-generation, reproduced over the generations in patrilineal perpetuity, that masculinity seeks to make a name for itself. "He," that ubiquitous male member, is the masculinist

signature writ large—the pronoun of the invisible man; the subject of the surveillant, sexual order; the object of humanity personified. It must be our aim not to deny or disavow masculinity, but to disturb its manifest destiny—to draw attention to it as a prosthetic reality—a "prefixing" of the rules of gender and sexuality; an appendix or addition, that willy-nilly, supplements and suspends a "lack-in-being."

—Homi Bhabha, "Are You a Man or a Mouse?" in Maurice Berger and Brian Wallis, *Constructing Masculinity* (1995)

And so the matador holds himself erect, his feet impeccably united, bound together by the fear of embarrassing himself before his audience, and also by the bandages wrapped snugly around his ankles, concealed by the vomit-pink stockings and by the glitter of his slippers. Rigidity of a man alone, rigidity of a sword. The muleta, slowly spread, covers with its eyelid the shaft of metal, all too visible, a chimerical spurt disgorged from a steel pupil.

—Michel Leiris, *Tauromachies* (1937)

At the end of the war in Kosovo, newspapers around the world published photographs of the British commander of NATO forces, Michael Jackson, describing him as a real macho, a visibly tough and determined man. War, as is always the case, brought to the forefront—along with the horrors and injustices—a type of man in uniform to whom we attribute characteristics of excessive masculinity. Machismo, for the most part, is not given a very positive connotation; the term, which comes from Mexican culture, has recently come to identify the full array of overbearing and overweening arrogance that accompanies male power around the world. At times, however, as in the case of Jackson, it would seem that public opinion can tolerate this sort of behavior. Unless, of course, we find the same sort of character in the enemy camp, which we then define as monstrous. "We need strong men," and military machismo can be thought

of as a continuation of other "masculine qualities" that are accepted in this contradictory manner.

The same thing seems to happen with the "cool" character of certain film archetypes, seen as a necessary dose of cold-bloodedness and cynicism, from Humphrey Bogart to James Bond. From the insensitive and violent Marlon Brando in *A Streetcar Named Desire*, to the tough old-fashioned men portrayed by John Wayne, to the ice-cold eyes of Clint Eastwood, or the pure cynicism of Harvey Keitel in *Bad Lieutenant*, we have a vast and varied collection of "rough manners" that all contributed to an image of a masculinity that is negative but almost necessary.

The English magazine *FHM* (For Him Magazine), newly published in France and targeting men only, based its launch campaign on the slogan "FHM, men are about to get a new bad habit…." The advertisements in the

Telly Savalas, as Detective Kojak, shaving

facing page:
Marlon Brando and Mary Murphy in *The Wild One*, 1954, directed by Laszlo Benedek

campaign show groups of men watching sports on television amid the litter of a take-out pizza dinner.

Historians and scholars of the nineteenth and twentieth centuries have explained that this vision of "masculinity" has its roots in the collective imagination that, in the nineteenth century, surrounded the "abnormal," be they reprobates, scoundrels, libertines, lady-killers, onanists, or heartbreakers.

Michel Foucault and Angus McLaren reconstructed this constellation of knavery as it appears in trials and medical and legal inquiries of the nineteenth century, when it was attributed to masculine weakness and immaturity, which were seen to engender pride, stubbornness, and villainy.

Classified as deviant by legal and medical thinkers, these cases formed a category to be distinguished from that of "gentlemen." This deviance, within which "abnormal" sexuality played a prominent role, forms the basis of a masculinity with "rough manners," which, even after the demise of the nineteenth century's courtrooms and madhouses, persists as a category of excess.

Novelists of the nineteenth century treated this sort of masculinity with a greater degree of subtlety than was to be found in normative discourse. But even Stendhal's antiheroes remind us of a type of man—born without privilege or means—who must avail himself of every sort of expedient to make his way in the world, and who is often condemned to failure precisely for his use of these expedients (in his *Barry Lyndon*, Stanley Kubrick portrayed such a figure). Males that want to rise in a world in which the weak simply do not survive are obliged to engage in a healthy dose of knavery.

In contrast to these "rough manners," the Victorian world invented the figure of "Peter Pan," a boy who refuses to grow up and who rejects any explicit manifestation of male sexuality. His eternal childhood saves him from having to transform his "impishness" into the behavior of a reprobate. Captain Hook is shown as an opposing model, where being bloody-minded is taken for being adult.

It seems that the male of the nineteenth-century imagination has no choices other than adolescence or excess. And the twentieth century appears to have offered him the same fate, at least in film and in television. Between James Dean's *Rebel Without a Cause* and the outlaws of Westerns, there is not a lot of room left to maneuver. Between the excess of "real men" and the inadequacy of "Peter Pans," a middle ground of masculinity, a "normal" masculinity, is invisible.

Historians of sexuality and customs have pointed out that the notion of masculinity (like that of femininity) is a relatively recent development. It is not thought to

Muhammad Alì, 1982. Photo by Ken Regan/ Camera 5

have evolved until the eighteenth century, after centuries of belief in a general resemblance between the sexual needs and emotions of men and women. It was not until the seventeenth century that physicians began to draw radical distinctions between what can be called the "opposite sexes." And, in reality, the term *sex* at first appears only in reference to women (for example, in the *Encyclopedia* of Diderot and d'Alembert).

Women's sexuality—the fact that a woman has a uterus—was proclaimed as important by scientists and philosophers, taken as an indication of the public and private roles for which "nature" meant to destine women.

The link of masculinity with sexuality was, on the other hand, greatly weakened. To quote from Rousseau's *Emile*: "The male is male only at certain moments. The female is female her whole life or at least during her whole youth."

Of course, ordinary people, as well as poets and authors, knew perfectly well even before the Enlightenment that there was a "difference," but this difference was not thought to be a "physical," "biological," "sexual difference, understood as a difference in sexual apparatus," but rather as a broader difference, less easily based on the specific physiological factors. Scholars nowadays call this difference "gender," in the sense that these are two different constellations—different in terms of language, practices, movements, dreams, and destinies—not merely based on a simple pair of opposites: male/female. The idea that was intrinsic in the division of labor, in everyday practices and in rituals, in music, dance, and literature was that these two worlds might intersect, but they could never merge.

Misunderstandings—whether tragic, like that between Desdemona and Othello, or comic, such as that between Harlequin and Columbine—provided a clear sign that there was no easy communication between the sexes, that male behavior and female behavior were substantially different.

The masculinity that emerged from the Industrial Revolution onward was more solitary, more vulnerable, and less solid. It attempted to model itself on a medical/biological/normative concept that had hitherto been reserved for women, perceived as the only "sex." Prior to this, the male was the "invisible sex," because the fact of being a man was not necessarily seen to be based on physiology (but rather on behavior, in the things a man does, in his practices). According to Thomas Laqueur in *Making Sex* (1990):

"The notion, so powerful after the eighteenth century, that there had to be something outside, inside, and throughout the body which defines male as opposed to female and which provides the foundation for an attraction of opposites is entirely absent from classical or Renaissance medicine. In terms of the millennial traditions of western medicine, genitals came to matter as the marks of sexual opposition only last week."

this and facing
page:
Festivals for
Saint Alfio, Saint
Cirino, and
Saint Filadelfo,
Sicily, Sixties and
Seventies.
Photos by
Enzo Sellerio

The transformation of the world of men into so many biologically male individuals was an operation that made a caricature of masculinity, turning it into rough manners. Men, in order to prove that they were male, had to emphasize their differences from women. To quote Laqueur again:

"To have a penis or not says it all in most circumstances, and one might for good measure add as many other differences as one chooses: women menstruate and lactate, men do not; women have a womb that bears children, and men lack both this organ and this capacity. I do not dispute any of these facts, although if pushed very hard they are not quite so conclusive as one might think. (A man is presumably still a man without a penis, and scientific efforts to fix sex definitively, as in the Olympic Committee's testing of the chromosomal configuration of buccal cavity cells, leads to ludicrous results.)"

In the absence of a clear and easy distinction, men avail themselves of rough manners. Males, in order to show that they are real men, must produce rowdy noise and make scenes—the roar of a Harley-Davidson, popping wheelies on a Vespa, a certain tone of voice. Otherwise, their "sex" remains invisible, dangerously neuter. Machismo, from this point of view, is a "negative" construct required to make males visible. As a Mexican proverb points out, either you are a macho, or you simply are nothing:

El macho vive mientras el cobardo quiere (The macho lives while the coward wishes he could). This is to say that there is no zero degree of masculinity: it is always excessive, hypertrophic, emphatic. Machismo, then, is the only way that men can be seen.

Apparently this tendency is not limited to sexualized societies like our own, wavering between the extreme importance attributed to the genitalia and the "Word from On High" of absolute sexual equality. Historians and anthropologists tell us that in other times and in societies quite different from ours—in societies where the world was or is still divided into two spheres of sharply distinct genders—the "male gender" needed somehow to emphasize itself in order to gain recognition. In these worlds males had to prove their maleness with numerous tests and demanding rituals of initiation. In the words of anthropologist K. E. Read, who for many years studied masculinity among the aboriginal

peoples of Papua New Guinea, "In the final analysis, the idea which men hold of themselves is based primarily on what men do rather than on what they have at birth. They recognize, indeed, that in physiological endowment men are inferior to women, and, characteristically, they have recourse to elaborate artificial means to redress the contradiction and to demonstrate its opposite."

It seems that many traditional societies share this belief. One becomes a man only by strenuously working to escape maternal influence. Adolescent males face an extremely difficult and painful passage. They must cancel from their bodies the "effeminate" influence of their mothers and the other women of their community, replacing them with "rough manners." Therefore, after weaning or at the threshold of adolescence they are taken from their mothers, and they are placed in the houses of the men, chambers where identity is forged. Here, adult men will subject them to violent and humiliating rituals.

Among the Sambia of New Guinea, who have been carefully studied in recent years by anthropologists and psychiatrists, boys must purge themselves of female humors. Adult males set an ambush for boys, pin them down, and then cause nosebleeds by inserting sharp canes and reeds in their nostrils. Blood, and much of the food that does not come from hunting, is considered to be a female substance and therefore a pollutant of masculinity. From the moment of the ambush until the young men take wives, they live in an exclusive and secret world of men alone, where they will learn to have monthly losses of blood (in order to purge themselves, but also in order to acquire the power of menstruation), to vomit, and to charge themselves with sperm—through fellatio—in order to provide a hedge against the danger that the women with whom they will have relations as adults will absorb all of their sperm. Sweating, fasting, and other physical ordeals to which they are subjected in the houses of the men last for many days. Along with these ordeals, the boys are awakened in the middle of the night and insulted regularly for being clumsy and generally inadequate.

It is a constellation where brutality replaces all other relationships. Is it not reminiscent of the sort of treatment offered in boot camp to raw recruits or the initiation rituals of urban gangs? The goal is to attain an implacable hardness, a relentless toughness. The criticism of young men's clumsiness and incompetence is a way of hammering out of them all vagueness, laziness, and sentimentality, and making them understand that masculinity is a quality that is always in danger, that men are always inadequate. Among the Sambia this training almost never results in homosexuality. Instead it serves to prepare young men for the truly difficult encounter that may deprive them of all their energies and even of their very masculinity: the encounter with women. Once he has become adult, a male who spends too much time with his wives is considered suspicious and effeminate. Frequent sexual intercourse is considered dangerous for men, presenting the potential risk of a loss of virility.

As Gilbert Herdt and Robert Stoller put it in their *Intimate Communications* (1990), "The ways men use their myths, plus their homosexual and heterosexual practices in creating and maintaining masculinity, belie the public ideology of the male cult: at its heart the myth speaks of men's deepest doubts that they are fully male. One's maleness and masculinity will fade away without ruthless, ritual defenses to preserve them."

Couldn't we use this same description, however, to explain many other constellations of masculinity? For instance, to give an account of the public ideologies and the rituals of power that have been used to keep women away from the sites of male exclusivity: the main square, the beer hall, political parties, and business. In many societies, these spaces are supposed to be kept clear of the unsettling presence of women by regulations designed to safeguard a male identity that is felt to be in continual danger in the face of another, more solid identity. It is as if male domination were merely the other face of female power.

For those who, like Pierre Bourdieu, have developed theories of male domination as being "a priori," this idea

comes as a blasphemy. According to Bourdieu, male arrogance is the source of everything else, including sexual differentiation, which he describes as nothing more than a form of inequality. In other words, the difference between the world of men and the world of women is merely an "ideology" that conceals a social injustice and an unfair distribution of resources. It is interesting to note that a response to this hypothesis has come recently from a number of women scholars, veterans or leaders of the feminist movements of the past thirty years, now beginning to deal with the question of the difference between the sexes. They have begun to wonder whether being male or being female is a biological reality or whether it is actually a cultural construct. These scholars suggest that the former distinction be described as "sexual" and the latter as "gender." In order to be men or women, it is not enough to be born with certain physical attributes; it is necessary to "become men or women socially." Lately, a great student of Levi-Strauss, Françoise Heritier, and an excellent anthropologist, Sherry Ortner, have set forth the idea that differences are a constant upon which all societies are based.

The idea is that the difference between two worlds, one called masculinity and the other femininity, has very little to do with physiological differences. Aside from recognition at birth—"It's a boy," "It's a girl!"—there is an entire construction that follows, and that is not taken for granted from the outset, beginning with the Western fascination with pink and blue that demonstrates that it is not enough to be born a boy or a girl but that it is also necessary to be swaddled in one of two different colors in order to be "distinguished." The idea that infants become men and women only through many different phases of testing and confirmation is found in various cultures. In many languages—including German—infants have no gender, and study of a coastal culture in Madagascar, the Vezo, confirms that infants are recognized as being "boys" or "girls" only after completing certain male or female practices, tasks, or rites.

The topic is extremely complex, and perhaps the question cannot be answered definitively: is the difference between men and women biological or cultural? Probably a biological foundation serves as a substrate for a further cultural division that makes the biological basis more or less significant. Here, the only thing one can do is to suggest a view of male "life," of male "experience" in our time, that is less of a caricature than what we have seen so far. The high quality and vast range of "feminist" scholarship, the creation of women's studies and gender studies, have all made it clear that there is a corresponding ignorance about men. We know little or nothing about

Make My Night 1998, multiple self-portrait. Photo by Paul M. Smith the formation of male identity; until now there has been little study of the practices of masculinity, excepting the "obvious" points that a necessarily excessive masculinity offered. As Laqueur points out: "It is probably not possible to write a history of man's body and its pleasures because the historical record was created in a cultural tradition where no such history was necessary."

We should remember that alongside machismo—or rough manners—is "Peter Pan" and what that implies: is a relic of primitive embarrassment, the response to an identity without adequate distinguishing features, an identity that runs not only the constant risk of slipping into vagueness, but one even more dire: into the great world of mothers. That is why men have to isolate themselves, frequenting only other men. In the southern part of Italy, especially, spending the long years of adolescence—on the street, at the little wall where the boys hung out, at the beach—in male company meant

men's anguish in the face of the necessity of proving that they are men; their awareness of the inadequacy of merely being a man in biological terms. Masculinity is a practice of inadequacy—and not only among the Sambia: you can never be masculine enough and if you are not sufficiently masculine then you are dangerously not male.

I remember a male world that relied upon separation in order to find confirmation "on its own." I grew up in Sicily. Masculinity at that time and in that place—it was a community of boys, adults, sailors, farmers, civilians, layabouts, and old men—expressed itself as a strange combination of boldness and isolation. The ostentation of masculinity, masculinity as a "proof," accepting a constant state of jeopardy. Aggression, ridicule, physical contact on the brink of homosexuality, as if to push the others to the extreme limit—where it is up to them to escape embarrassment: all of these things served to "roughen" young men, to teach them manners that would clearly show that they were not female. One became male "jerkily," reacting to and never escaping the physical embarrassment of adolescence. A real male is a bit awkward, rough, tough with his body. If he remains graceful—Peter Pan, who could fly—or rounded in his movements, then he would remain in sweet childhood, dreaming in his mother's lap. He must lose that "grace"; he must become "graceless," "disgraceful."

It is a long training that serves to redefine and shape one's physicality, a rough game and one that takes its toll. But in this game a difference is constructed and emphasized, a difference that at first is extremely slight. In this rough game, in this turmoil, the individual body—the individual male body—does not exist and must be brought to life.

A piazza in a small town in Sicily in the Seventies. Three men, photographed by Enzo Sellerio, look into the lens in a daring, challenging manner. All three of them —hand or hands on their hips, thumb tucked under or resting upon their belt, the weight of their bodies leaning unevenly on one or the other of their legs, their torsos twisting slightly—take positions that seem to communicate at once a sense of "alert" and at the same time of repose, as if to say, "let's see what happens." Here, too, there is no single body, but a cluster of bodies assuming the same pose. Likewise, their gazes, their faces, their clothing are component parts of a reciprocal mimesis. Being men and showing that they are men seems to be the same thing, forming a common front, an acquired (made, however, to look "natural") capacity to appear. The male body exists only as a collective body—as a body that imitates other bodies around it, beside it. If a male body is alone, it risks implosion, it risks becoming a ridiculous body that alone cannot justify itself because it is only a sex, or perhaps we should say a quasi-sex.

Jacques Lacan (in "La Signification du phallus," a seminar from 1958) says that every display of virility becomes, per se, feminine. Could this be the reason that every photograph of men's fashion with a male model seems vaguely embarrassing? And could this be why male nudity in fashion photography necessarily seems to be created for a homosexual audience? As if, in fact, the individual male body was not made to be "shown" (for there is no history of the female gaze upon the male body). The male body, displayed, is immediately a body that passes from invisibility to the female orientation of the sex.

There is a physical shame of being male that is manifested in the cultures of the South. It can be seen in a pattern of casual contact between male bodies, a contact that is sought out in the group and then avoided in terms of its possible emotional consequences. It is a shame that derives from an acquired ignorance—a real man should not "know" about his own body, he cannot have a complete identification with it, but only an angular relationship, rough and graceless.

Good Friday, Palermo: a dozen men cluster together to carry a statue of Our Lady of Sorrows. Two by two, under the incredible weight of an entire church altar mounted on two long poles—chest to chest, cheek to cheek—they walk along like a single strange animal.

They are all dressed alike, in the white smocks of the confraternity, and they move the erect, weeping statue of the Madonna with an undulating motion that reveals the intensity of the effort. Their concerted effort makes this single colony-like body strange and yet at the same time justifies their collective embrace. There is an extreme complicity and an enormous embarrassment in the close contact of these male bodies. This same scene, this same phallophoria, can be found on Good Friday in other parts of Sicily, in Puglia, in Andalusia, and in Greece.

It is interesting to note that both here and in the cultures studied by anthropologists (the Sambia, for instance) masculinity is only established among males. The relationship with the female gaze and with the feminine world is something that is established only after the individual "emerges" from the male group and encounters a woman. The male group does not interact with the female group, one world does not view the other. (Perhaps this is why, no matter how far we may be from cultures in which the difference was extreme—and how can we deny that the difference remains powerful, quotidian, and concealed in all of the folds of our gestures—there is still a lack of study of masculinity.) Fashion offers a clear demonstration of the isolation of the male. Men's clothing serves to "cover," not "uncover," the male, it serves to conceal him in the regularity of the uniform, which establishes him in a brotherhood of other males and in the silence of the outfit. If an outfit works to "display" the male, this individual single male, then there is always the risk mentioned in the quote that appears at the beginning of this essay. The torero, dressed in vomit-pink stockings and glittering slippers, is—if he fails to kill the bull, if he doesn't stab him with his sword, if he doesn't (as Leiris puts it) stab him between the breasts—just a bit ridiculous: a Peter Pan who justifies his excessive femininity with the presence of a sword.

Palermo, Sferracavallo: with a female friend, I watch a group of men at dinner in a restaurant. They are holding a very spirited discussion. They seem to be quarreling, but in fact they are "disputing"; indeed, they are disputing who has the floor, who can speak. The man who has the floor at the moment stands up and leans toward his chosen listener with his entire body: he ridicules him, he challenges him, he dares him to answer back. Others break in. The same process each time. Later, we discover (because the men come to offer an explanation, "embarrassed because we were watching them") that they are a group of street sweepers who work the night shifts. There are disagreements to be resolved between the sweepers on the early night shift and the others, who work the late night shift. They see each other briefly each night when their shifts change but they never have enough time to settle certain work-related problems. And so they decided to meet for

dinner. Their "dispute" is a staging of a physical ritual, a setting forth of excess that is in turn met with another helping of excess, always precisely to the limit beyond which things would quickly degenerate: by nearly hurling themselves one at each other they achieve a form of physical recomposition of the social body; but we are there, we see them, we embarrass them. This sort of staging of masculinity cannot admit an outsider's gaze. Masculinity, even collective masculinity, is not something to be put on show. It is meant to be consumed strictly in the interior of the group.

Perhaps these street sweepers were seeking an answer to the question, what is masculinity and how do we express it? Masculinity is a destiny. Destiny is an agreement to be reached, perhaps, at the end of this or other dinners (the Last Supper was a stag dinner). Yes, masculinity is a destiny—and perhaps for this reason it is less natural than femininity. Masculinity —whatever it may mean—is a suspension, not in the temporal sense, but in the more physical, elastic sense. It appears in the gesture of the torero or a *capoeira* dancer, in a rush, an "élan," a spurt—for that matter, flicker or jet was one of the names of Dionysus—that will sometimes fall short.

Yul Brynner

facing page:
Clint Eastwood,
Magnum Force,
1973, directed by
Ted Post. Photo by
Philippe Halsman

Ted Polhemus

THE INVISIBLE MAN

Style and the Male Body

For centuries the men of the Nuba tribe of the Sudan have spent several hours a day, every day, painting intricate designs on their naked bodies and sculpting their hair into fantastic styles that would be the envy of any punk. At night they sleep with their heads supported on special racks so as not to disturb their hairstyles. Few, if any, tribal peoples would find this extraordinary. Indeed, the universality of the Peacock Male amongst traditional cultures suggests that it is an extremely ancient component of human development. So too within that moment which we identify as "Western history": from ancient Egypt, Greece, or Rome right up until only a century or two ago European men were preening themselves with great care and exhibiting their physicality with great pride.

So what happened? J. C. Flugel, in *The Psychology of Clothes* (1930), identifies this marked shift away from masculine adornment and pride in male physicality as the Great Masculine Renunciation and pointedly underlines its historical significance: "men may be said to have suffered a great defeat in the sudden reduction of male sartorial decorativeness which took place at the end of the eighteenth century. At about that time there occurred one of the most remarkable events in the whole history of dress, one under the influence of which we are still living, one, moreover, which has attracted far less attention than it deserves: men gave up their right to all the brighter, gayer, more elaborate, and more varied forms of ornamentation, leaving these entirely to the use of women, and thereby making their own tailoring the most austere and ascetic of the arts . . . [In this] man abandoned his claim to be considered beautiful. He henceforth aimed at being only useful. So far as clothes remained of importance to him, his utmost endeavours could lie only in the direction of being 'correctly' attired, not of being elegantly or elaborately attired."

Flugel lays the blame for this sad event on the French Revolution. Because such elaborate male attire had previously served also to mark out aristocratic privilege (and given that it was of course men rather than women who ultimately exercised this privilege) the democratization of the social order that followed in the wake of the French Revolution understandably shifted away from fancy, elitist male attire. This was particularly true in England, where the upper classes, eager to avoid the same fate as their French counterparts, moved quickly to embrace a style that signaled sobriety, responsibility, and hard work rather than frivolity, privilege, and leisure.

Although clearly correct, Flugel's analysis does not, however, go far enough. It seems obvious, for example,

Young Dinka tribesmen, Sudan. Photo by George Rodger

that the experience of Britain and other European powers in the Age of Imperialism must have further fortified the Great Masculine Renunciation: eager to distance themselves from the tribal and peasant peoples that they subjugated, European colonialists literally embodied their presumed superiority in their "rational" and "civilized" appearance, in contrast to the "primitive" body decorations and "absurd" frivolity of non-European male style.

Then, the final nail in the coffin of the Western peacock came in the form of the Industrial Revolution. Whereas throughout human history *Homo habilis*—man the maker of objects—had needed physical as well as mental acuteness, now the physical aspect of production was taken over by machines. Thus it came to pass that success and power came to be increasingly associated with mental ability and less with physical dexterity.

While the effects of the Great Masculine Renunciation can be seen most clearly and vividly in the realm of male appearance—with male Western style coming to focus exclusively on what the fashion historian James Laver termed the Hierarchy Principle, where dress and adornment serve only to signal wealth and power—it is on an ontological level that its effects are most profound and disturbing. Although Descartes may have delineated a dualism of mind and body (which I expect any traditional, non-Westernized peoples would see as extremely bizarre), he did not dismiss the physical form as an irrelevant appendage of human existence. But as the Industrial Revolution blossomed and took hold as an all-encompassing worldview, being—the location of the self—came increasingly to be seen as cerebral rather than physical. Mary Shelley's *Frankenstein* takes the first steps in this direction by rehousing a being-soul-mind in a new body. It is but a short step from this kind of thinking to that science fiction that has human brains happily bubbling away in glass beakers—or, now in real life, that has wealthy individuals cryogenically freezing their heads for posterity while leaving the rest of their bodies (now obviously seen as ontologically insignificant) to rot. On a more widespread level, here too is the computer "nerd," whose body only survives on junk food and inactivity while he (and it is almost always he) lives out life in electronic virtual reality—perhaps even representing himself as a digital "avatar" whose physical form (and even gender) may have absolutely no relationship to his "real" (now = unreal) body.

The implications of Western man (now, of course, virtually all men on our planet) becoming The Invisible Man—a cerebral being unencumbered by physiological form—are all pervasive and breathtaking. Unable to take pride in and express himself through his body, The Invisible Man sought and achieved greater control over the bodies of women—to convert the female form into a surrogate body for that most ancient form of self-expression which he could no longer effect. (The feminists' cry of "Our Bodies Ourselves" surfacing in the Sixties as a belated response to this corporal colonialism.) But, inevitably, this strategy brought Western/Westernized man more frustration than satisfaction: its failure evident in the high incidence and cultural significance of male > female transvestism (and also male fetishism, in which an item of female apparel is imbued with magical, exclusive erotic force).

My own view is that a—perhaps *the*—key problem facing our culture today is masculine confusion, frustration, lack of identity, purpose, and personal pride. And furthermore, central to this problem is that estrangement from the body and its ancient, fundamental medium of expression that modern man brought upon himself when he decided that he should become a sublime, disembodied intelligence (but, of course, with an attached, massive and fully functioning penis).

It is wrong, however, to suggest that all men in the West succumbed to the presumption that a "Real Man" is ipso facto an invisible man. The Great Masculine Renunciation was focused upon the middle and upper classes of northern Europe (and then America), it was more suited to Protestant than Catholic sensibilities, and was, of course, exclusively white. Never anything like a demographic majority, it was, however, precisely this group that constituted the unchallenged power base of nineteenth-century life throughout the world. Thus, riding on the wave of the Industrial Revolution, colonial influence, and Western missionary zeal, this minority's physiologically estranged and sartorially inhibited model of masculinity became the norm from Africa to Asia—indeed, anywhere where men sought power, prestige and wealth.

From the Age of Colonialism until the present day, to be taken seriously on the world stage, a political or business leader must first renounce his physicality and hide his body behind that now universal uniform of the Invisible Man—the bland, ill-fitting suit.

Ironically, however, while the Great Masculine Renunciation has been spreading across the globe, its validity has increasingly been challenged within the West. Indeed, it could be argued that the driving force behind Western popular culture in the twentieth century has been the reassertion of male physicality. Tapping precisely into those segments of Western society that had refused to be drawn into the Great Masculine Renunciation—the working class; Mediterranean Europe and (also Catholic) Central and Southern America; the Wild West; the Black populations of the Caribbean, Europe, and America; homosexual culture; youth—twentieth-century popular culture directly confronted the sad, emasculated legacy of the Invisible Man. Consider just a few snapshots from this complex history . . .

The Latin Lovers of the early cinema;

The dance crazes of the Twenties and Thirties, such as the tango or the jitterbug, which derived either from Latin or Black culture;

The tight-jeaned physicality of both the good and the bad guys in the Western cinema genre;

The rough, uninhibited sexuality of Marlon Brando and other cinema actors in their portrayal of working class males;

The Black and youthful roots of rock and roll's liberation of male sexuality;

The masculine focus of postwar, youth-oriented street style: zooties, bikers, hipsters, teddy boys, mods, rockabillies, surfers, rude boys, psychedelics, hippies, skinheads, glam rockers, rastas, headbangers, skaters, punks, new romantics, goths, B boys—all more significant for their effect on male than female style;

The abiding and over-riding stylistic influence of the American, British, and Caribbean Black male on popular music;

From swinging London to disco to house, the mainstreaming of gay culture (with its positive assertion of male physicality and its delight in sartorial exuberance) into straight society;

The tattoo renaissance, which has swept across America and Europe to give new respect to an art form which was previously in the West seen only as a sign of moral and social failure;

And the phenomenal rise of body piercing, which so directly and unashamedly celebrates that tribal peacock that the Great Masculine Renunciation of the West sought to brand as barbaric, backward, artless, and unworthy of respect.

The interesting point in all this is that it is precisely those social groups and cultural institutions that retained a positive vision of the male body and its decoration that

Easter in Sicily, Festival of the Living Man, in Ribera. Photo by Franco Zecchin have thrived within the context of twentieth-century popular culture. Surely this is not simply coincidence. Nor, I would argue, is the fact that what is particularly striking and unique about the twentieth century is its ever elevated respect for the popular at the expense of elitist "high" culture. In this we have brought to the fore the key struggle of our age: not that between high and popular culture, but rather, more precisely, that between disembodiment and a concept of self which embraces and rejoices in male physicality.

But while our popular culture has long provided a wide range of mythic prototypes of just such masculine embodiment—Valentino, John Wayne, Brando, Marcello Mastroianni, Elvis Presley, James Brown, Mick Jagger, David Bowie, Michael Jackson, Marilyn Manson, and so forth—our break away from The Great Masculine Renunciation has proved more difficult in real life.

In the heady days of the mid-Sixties, however, it seemed as if this too was about to change. Typically the direct descendants of those who had first embarked on the Great Masculine Renunciation, the hippies and psychedelic freaks of America and Britain launched a Unisex Revolution that seemed set to topple once and for all the supremacy of the Invisible Man. Suddenly males as well as females could grow their hair long, wear bright colors, and paint designs on their bodies (at least at pop festivals). But while, undoubtedly, unisex did have a sustained, positive effect on male appearance, its most marked and general effect was ironically to bring females, too, within that renunciation of finery, fancy dress, and the cosmetic arts to which, previously, only males had succumbed. In brief, instead of men wearing make-up, perming their hair and showing off their legs in short skirts, the Unisex Revolution brought a new generation of women who (unlike their mothers in the Fifties) saw no need to wear makeup, let their hair grow naturally, and dressed casually in jeans and T-shirts. Instead of males embracing "finery" (to use Flugel's phrase), females often chose to reject it.

But as a depressing army of "scruffy" hippies spread out across and beyond America, the early Seventies saw a dramatic reawakening of flamboyance and physical assertiveness amongst urban Black American males. As if to remind whites that they had never willingly subscribed to The Great Masculine Renunciation, the children of the zooties and the bebopping hipsters conjured up that most awesome

48

Club En Femme, London, 1996. Photo by John Londei, London

display of peacock power that was first known as The Pimp Look and then gained greater recognition in the form of Funk. In his essay "Funk Chic," from *Mauve Gloves & Madmen, Clutter & Vine* (1977), the American writer Tom Wolfe looked on spell-bound at . . .

"All the young aces and dudes out there lollygagging around the front of the Monterey Club [in New Haven, Connecticut] wearing their two-tone patent Pyramids with the five-inch heels that swell out at the bottom to match the Pierre Chareau Art Deco plaid bell-bottom baggies they have on with the three-inch-deep elephant cuffs tapering upwards toward the 'spray-can fit' in the seat, as it is known, and the peg-top waistband with self covered buttons and the beagle-collar pattern-on-pattern Walt Frazier shirt, all of it surmounted by the mid-length leather piece with the welted waist seam and the Prince Albert pockets and the black Pimpmobile hat with the four-inch turn-down brim and the six-inch pop-up crown with the golden chain-belt hatband ... and all of them, every ace, every dude, out there just getting over in the baddest possible way, come to play and dressed to slay."

Spurred on in equal measure by admiration for this dazzling new Black assertion of peacock power and disdain for that boring antistyle that had become the uniform of the hippies, it was the birth of glam rock in Britain that gave white males another chance at re-discovering their bodies and their physical expressiveness. The visual legacy of David Bowie, Marc Bolan, and all the other glam rockers who followed in their platform-heeled footsteps cannot be overestimated. Through punk, the new romantics, the goths and heavy metal, the idea that white males too could be flamboyantly attired, physically assertive, erotically charged peacocks lived on. And not only on the stage or at rock festivals: on the street or at nightclubs young (and not so young) straight white males were openly strutting their funky stuff. Then, as disco brought gay influences into the mix, it seemed clear that The Invisible Man was rapidly becoming an endangered species.

And yet, as we approach the end of the twentieth century, what is striking is the extraordinary extent to which the Invisible Man continues to thrive—the failure rather than the success of our popular culture's attempt to roll back the Great Masculine Renunciation. For at least in terms of mainstream, middle-class, white male style, it is often hard to believe that the Unisex Revolution, glam, punk, the new romantics and disco ever happened. For when in the late Eighties the smoke of all these popular culture explosions cleared, the lads down the pub or cracking open a six-pack for the Superbowl were not really all that sartorially different from their forefathers: perhaps a bit more stylishly, expensively

dressed, more casual in their appearance, but hardly Ziggy Stardust and the Spiders from Mars.

This fact is most evident when we compare the dramatic changes that have come about in accepted female style in the last fifty years with those that have been witnessed in male style within the same time period. Today, even in the workplace, let alone at the supermarket or in her leisure time, it is a rare woman who is not able to wear styles that only a generation or two ago were seen exclusively as "masculine" (trousers, "sensible" footwear or hairstyles, no visible makeup, denim jeans and work wear, and so forth). Indeed, unlike her grandmother, today's woman needs to accept few if any gender specific proscriptions on her appearance (even that one surviving preserve of masculine body decoration, the tattoo, having now gone unisex).

Not so her male contemporary, however. While arguably more free to wear different colors and styles than his grandfather, a "normal" male of today is still rigorously precluded from adopting any number of looks that are still categorized as "female only": visible make-up, skirts or dresses, see-through fabrics, exotic hairstyles, and (except when engaged in sports) tight-fitting, body-shape-revealing garments. Thirty years ago in *Modesty & Dress* the fashion historian James Laver pronounced that the function of men's apparel is to signal hierarchy/status/wealth; while the function of female attire is to promote sexual attraction. When I see men in nightclubs wearing Armani suits chatting up women who are dressed as if for the beach, when I note how rarely one sees a couple where he is wearing tighter jeans or shorter shorts than she is, when I see today's male Black pop musicians content to display their gold jewelry and designer labels while leaving it to skimpily clad female dancers to provocatively display their bodies, I wonder if—depressingly—James Laver's dictum holds today the same truth that it did thirty years ago.

Since the Seventies onward feminists have rightly battled for women to be seen as more than sex objects. At the same time, however, at least within the context of straight, mainstream society, the right of men to become sex objects has not been championed. Compared to the female form, the male body remains significantly undervalued. Fact: there are no male supermodels. Fact: almost all women's and men's magazines have pictures of women on their covers. Fact: male models, strippers, and porn stars are all paid considerably less than their female counterparts. So, while women have moved forward in their rightful claim to be valued for more than just their physicality, men—at least in straight, conventional society—are still typically valued only for that which could be more efficiently accomplished by a wired-up brain bubbling away in a glass beaker. (And that which one expects a future generation of Pentium processors will handle with ease).

And we take this state of affairs for granted—as if it were a condition of nature that the female body is more valuable, desirable, and exhibitable than that of a male. Thankfully we know from history and from anthropology that this is not the case. Western man's renunciation of his own physicality created a dangerous imbalance, a disfunction at the very core of our culture. The twentieth century has tried, but largely failed, to overcome this ontological estrangement. Let us hope that the twenty-first century sees fit to place the problem at the top of its agenda. For the Invisible Man—so lacking in expressiveness and self-respect, so full of pent-up rage and envy—is a danger to us all.

Andrea Balestri, Marco Ricchetti

MANUFACTURING MEN'S WEAR
Masculine Identity in the Structure of the Fashion Industry

Male and Female vs. Unisex

The distinction between men's wear and women's wear (or between men and women) has determined the structure and continues to guide the activities of the sectors of the economy that manufacture personal consumer goods: apparel, footwear, leather goods, jewelry, and cosmetics. This basic dichotomy permeates the very organization of the manufacturing processes; it affects the strategies of individual companies and corporations; it marks the language and imagery of advertising; it is intrinsic to many professional definitions, both new and old. And it constitutes a foundation of the way in which the final products are presented in the marketplace.

In all of these sectors, gender distinctions have proven to be extremely durable, capable up to now of withstanding, if not ignoring entirely, the larger currents that are moving our society toward a more general gender blindness. The steady drift toward informality, globalization, a general standardization of distribution networks, the sudden skyrocketing of business volume in virtual emporia, the ineluctable triumph of carefully crafted trademarks—all these currents gradually undermine businesses that have been painstakingly built on such factors as manual skill, practical knowledge, and commercial relationships built up over many decades.

Certain countries continue to hold positions of global leadership in apparel manufacture even though their costs of labor and goods might appear to be potentially unfavorable to specializing in apparel products, and this has long been the object of interest and study. Overall, however, not a great deal of attention has been paid to the varied historical, technical, and cultural factors and the specific approaches that underlie the production of men's wear and accessories, on the one hand, and women's wear and accessories, on the other.

The two extremes—men's wear/women's wear—that typified, in one way or another, the ateliers of tailors, have shaped the entire history of the apparel industry. The transformation of the leading crafts tailors into apparel manufacturing companies organized according to the standards of modern industry took place, for the most part, following the Second World War. Prior to 1950, nearly all apparel in Europe was produced either by crafts tailors or else in the home. From the very beginning of the development of the manufacturing sector, however, there was a distinctive juxtaposition of two parallel universes (manufacturing apparel for one gender or the other) where products, patterns, manufacturing techniques, seasons, and innovations moved forward incrementally, one sector leapfrogging the other, at times colliding, but never merging.

In France the development of the modern apparel industry coincided with the debut of a men's wear apparel

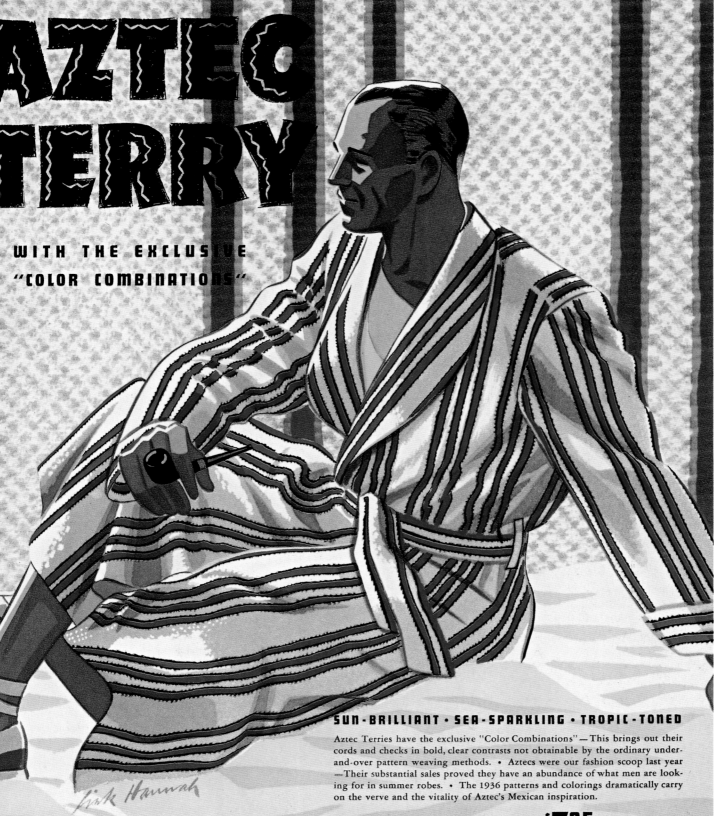

AZTEC TERRY

WITH THE EXCLUSIVE "COLOR COMBINATIONS"

SUN-BRILLIANT · SEA-SPARKLING · TROPIC-TONED

Aztec Terries have the exclusive "Color Combinations"—This brings out their cords and checks in bold, clear contrasts not obtainable by the ordinary under-and-over pattern weaving methods. • Aztecs were our fashion scoop last year —Their substantial sales proved they have an abundance of what men are looking for in summer robes. • The 1936 patterns and colorings dramatically carry on the verve and the vitality of Aztec's Mexican inspiration.

AZTEC BEACH and LOUNGE ROBES **$7⁹⁵** *Retail*

VAN BAALEN, HEILBRUN & CO.

Robes and House Jackets for Men and Boys

9 BROADWAY, NEW YORK   SAN FRANCISCO OFFICE: 341 MARKET STREET

VALENTINO

Valentino,
fall/winter
1999/2000
advertising
campaign.
Photo by
Steven Meisel

54

house, the Belle Jardinière, between 1820 and 1830. Mass-produced women's wear was not to make its appearance in Paris until several decades later.

In Italy, as well, the early stages of the industrialization of apparel manufacturing were clearly defined: the first companies in the sector to be established in Milan and Turin toward the end of the nineteenth century specialized in linen and shirts for men. GFT, a company that has been a leading manufacturer in the field of Italian men's wear for more than half a century, was founded in 1930 on the ruins of a small, existing concern.

It was not until after the Second World War that mass-production of women's wear began, in the years in which the earliest ancestors of the sector began operations: APEM of Vimodrone, Rosier of Milan, and Max Mara of Reggio Emilia. A milestone in the history of Italian fashion came with the decision (1953) on the part of the Manifattura Lane Gaetano Marzotto—which until that time had been limited to the production of woolen yarns and fabrics—to undertake a vertical integration, with a new division for the manufacture of men's wear.

In the more androgynous climate of the last few decades, many new entries in the arenas of apparel (practically all of the players in the Italian star system: Benetton, Stefanel, Diesel, Zara, and Replay) have produced and distributed, without distinction, men's wear and women's wear. This marks a clear break from the

previous manufacturing tradition, where a sharp orientation toward men's wear (Lubiam, Corneliani, Zegna, or Pal Zileri in Italy; Hugo Boss in Germany) or women's wear (Vestebene, Les Copains, Jenny, Max Mara) can be detected in every detail of corporate life, from purchasing to design, from research to advertising.

Two Industrial Cultures

The development of the fashion system as we know it today, in many countries, has been anything but linear. It is the same exuberant and unpredictable energy, at times incomprehensible, that we find in accounts of Italian apparel fairs. The factors that divide the two sectors go well beyond matters of the variations in cut or color as determined by social codes. Nor is it solely, or even primarily, a matter of the physical characteristics or different functions in the use of apparel. The dichotomy between men's wear and women's wear is one of the variables, along with the place in the pyramid of the "paths of fashion" or the axis of the "classic-innovative," that still primarily differentiates retail sales outlets, and that, hence, affects the various activities upstream of those retail sales outlets: trade fairs, specialty magazines, buying practices of wholesalers, divisions of the major apparel manufacturers, and modern distribution. Even the complex rituals of the collections are distinguished by patterns and schedules that are quite different for men's

eXTē

Exté,
spring/summer
1999 advertising
campaign. Photo
by Michelangelo
Di Battista

wear and women's wear; so great are these differences that, in several of the most important trade fairs, the industries have chosen to present women's wear in Milan and men's wear in Florence.

The tendency of geographical locations to specialize in this or that form of production is quite common, and reputations endure in the face of rapid change. This is true for London which, in the collective perception, is still often thought of as the capital of the men's wear industry, even though the statistics of international trade offer a slightly different view of things, showing Italy solidly in first place. Aside from what market shares may tell us, there is always a bit of truth in commonplaces like the above, and if it is true that the world is changing fast and the geography of industry is shifting, the accumulated skills and the images of excellence, once conquered, remain and endure.

If we consider lifestyles, the organization of life in modern societies, and the different conditions in which men and women live and work, there is nothing really surprising about the subdivision between men's wear and women's wear. Two systems of demand, two different markets—men's wear and women's wear—correspond to two different systems of supply, and it really couldn't be any different. If anything, what is surprising is the limited attention paid by economists and analysts of corporate organization to the specific features of the two sectors.

Even in the case of partially finished goods like

textiles, to which one cannot always easily attribute a specific use, the dichotomies between men's wear and women's wear are easy to detect. In general, here the boundaries between production for one or the other use are more nuanced: indeed, most of the threads and yarns and a portion of the supply of fabrics (such as denim, for instance) are used without distinction in apparel and knitwear for both men and women. But those are exceptions to a more general rule.

The history of the Italian woolen industry, for instance, has run along, and continues to run along, two different parallel tracks, consisting of "drapery" (fabrics for men's wear) and "woolens" (fabrics for women's wear). This is a complex distinction linked to the fibers utilized ("carded" wools in the first case, "combed" wools in the second), the manufacturing techniques (two different systems of spinning and finishing), and the intrinsic characteristics of the articles sold.

In tailored apparel for women, one uses (and, more important, there is a history of using), for the most part, fabrics made with carded wool, with patterns and colors that could in no case be used in men's wear. Something similar happens, on a smaller scale, in the production of silk fabrics, where printed articles are generally destined for use in women's wear; indeed, the printing of fabrics for ties is a sharply separate area of production.

In the multidimensional geography of the fashion marketplace, then, men's wear and women's wear

GIORGIO ARMANI

56

together represent a system of coordinates that constitutes the two hemispheres, different in terms of timing and phases in the creation and design of products, in terms of manufacturing process, in terms of the key characteristics that define product quality and make a certain outfit capable of satisfying the needs, desires, and dreams of the consumer.

In this imaginary map of fashion, the farthest extreme in the axis of men's wear is formal attire, or tailored clothing, which has been—for over a century, from the foundation of the ready-to-wear garment industry in the first few decades of the nineteenth century right up until the Seventies and Eighties of the twentieth century— along with work clothing, men's wear by definition.

The reasons for the split between the two markets are not difficult to reconstruct. All one need do is enter a clothing shop—actually, two different clothing shops, a men's wear shop and a women's wear shop—and observe the behavior of a male consumer and a female consumer.

When a male consumer needs to purchase, say, a suit or an unmatched jacket-and-trouser set, he will consider primarily (and just a few years ago, exclusively) the factors of wearability, fit, and comfort: every man has conducted the classic test-gesture of raising his arms like airplane wings and then bending his elbows. Next comes the quality of the fabric (lightness, softness) and the quality of the construction (precision of the stitching, strength, geometric precision of the checks or stripes of the fabric). The choices concerning the style, the color, and the accessories are minor variants, and are often suggested or guided by the shop owner or salesman.

Now let us step into a women's wear shop: the picture changes radically, the choice is made by the female consumer, based primarily on visual considerations, observing the overall look of the cut, color, fabric, or combination of fabrics, and is functional to the combination with various accessories. Secondary consideration is paid to wearability, the quality of details and finish, the precision of the fit; it is no accident that the number of sizes found in women's wear is usually no higher than 3-6, and often each manufacturer presents its own interpretation of sizes; moreover, there are practically no differences in terms of height.

The consequences of this dichotomy in behavior over the short arc of time preceding the decision to purchase and the customer's transaction at the cash register are pervasive, and they influence the entire structure of the organization of production.

The work involved in designing a new line of men's clothing (we are using the definition of men's clothing here as an extension of tailored clothing, a semantic extension that was valid almost universally until just a few decades ago and that today, as we shall see below, requires certain qualifications) is based on the subtle variations that need to be made on the overall silhouette in order to comply with the trends of the coming season, by

CERRUTI

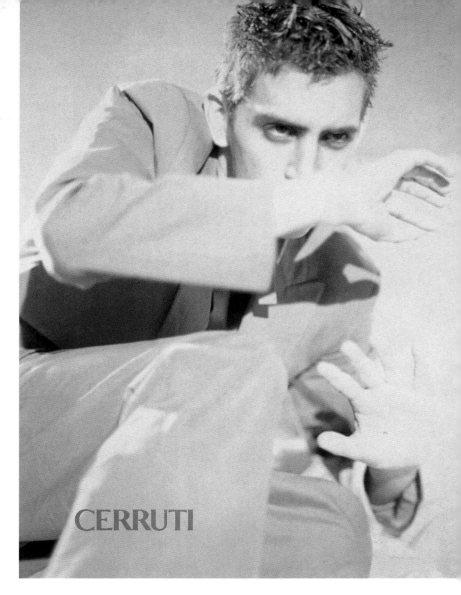

CERRUTI

lengthening or shortening the jacket or the cuffs, an increase or reduction of the padding in the shoulders, moving the buttons up or down, and so on, with intensely focused attention on the consequences of each and every change in terms of wearability and on the development of the various sizes. Once changes are made in the overall silhouette, work begins on selecting the assortment of fabrics, usually quite a broad array. Then prototypes are produced of the main variants of fabrics to be used in the sample arrays, while a single swatch is produced of most of the fabric variants to be shown to buyers (or else, through computer-assisted design, pictures of the item in a number of variants are developed and shown).

There is a different approach to the design of women's wear, where the product manager responsible for the development of the line works on the general orientation of style and themes for the upcoming season: colors, threads and yarns, fabrics, patterns, and accessories are developed with a unified approach. The variants on fabrics for a single model are few, often limited to the color.

The manufacturing process for men's wear is particularly long and complex, more so than for women's wear: the system of sizes is complicated by the proliferation of combinations of height, configuration, and drop, in an attempt to give the consumer the sensation of a custom-sewn product; the sewing operations require greater care (and may result in a higher percentage of

items discarded due to defects) especially when the fabrics feature striped or checkered patterns, in order to ensure precision in the matching and geometric precision of the left-hand and right-hand halves; a greater number of manual operations are required for the production of a structured item and for the construction of internal and external pockets; even after cutting and assembly, the manufacturing process proceeds slowly—the application of linings, prepressing, and pressing are all operations of considerable importance for the final wearability of the clothing, its overall quality, and customer satisfaction.

These are all the ingredients needed to prompt the companies, the organizational models, and the general structures of the industry itself to take diverging directions. Men's wear manufacturers tend to be more highly structured, less willing to subcontract phases of production to outside workshops; quality control over all the phases of production in which precision and tailoring skill are fundamental factors requires them to maintain plants, workers, and production within the company walls.

In terms of company balance sheets, this translates into sharply higher levels of sales volume per employee in women's wear than in men's wear, as you can see in the chart (p. 58), where we compare Italian companies that lead the two sectors. The selection of the companies that appear in the chart was not accidental, since—as always—the world of fashion resists all efforts to classify it clearly; we ruled out the *maisons* of the designers,

MEN'S WEAR

WOMEN'S WEAR

	1800
	1500
	1200
	900
	600
	300
	0

Canali · Inco · IAC · Ermenegildo Zegna · Sanremo · Forali · Hitman · Corneliani · Redaelli · Nervesa · Lubiam · Ciro Paone · Cantarelli · Brioni · Maska · Genny Moda · Columbus Mode · Pepper Industries · BVM · Fashion Box · Blufin · Marina Rinaldi · Alberto Aspesi · Textura · Marella · Max Mara

where much of the income derives from licensing or non-textile activities; we also ruled out such champions of Italian industry as Marzotto or Miroglio, because the textile factor is such a major component of their overall volume. The result is a list of midsized companies specializing in formal men's wear and women's wear.

The smaller range of variability of the products, the longer and more complex manufacturing cycles, however, generated greater economies of scale in the men's wear industry, which tends to be more greatly concentrated, with a smaller number of companies competing for the market, often with the weapon—here more powerful and effective than in the field of women's wear—of established and well-known trademarks.

When in an Industrial District . . .

Another interesting phenomenon linked to the differentiation of men's wear and women's wear sectors can be found in the geography of manufacturing, which is sharply localized within individual countries to areas that are homogeneous in terms of economic fundamentals.

A significant example of this trend can seen in the Italian apparel industry, which is distributed territorially (over Italy's proverbial hundred municipalities) in a series of centers that, in some cases, have specialized in the manufacture of products for women and, in other cases, for men. The dichotomy, mentioned above, between

woolens and drapery has developed in an almost paradigmatic fashion in Prato and Biella, two of Italy's leading textile centers.

The origins of this market specialization can be traced back to very particular circumstances. The use, once quite common in the wool mills of Prato, of recycled wools (rags) with relatively weak yarn resulted in textiles that were better suited for use in items, such as dresses or overcoats, which were not subjected to excessive stresses and strains. The virgin wools used by the competitors in the Biella region made it possible to create finer and stronger yarns, and were therefore used in the production of trousers and suits for men.

It is interesting, at this point, to note the way in which, around these technical characteristics, two different industrial cultures developed over time. Nowadays, the limitations that originally conditioned the distinct market alignments have vanished, but the consistency, rigor, and classical taste of Biella continues to appear in the region's production of fabrics for men's tailored clothing.

The focus, the flexibility, and the imagination of the people of Prato allowed them to develop the more fanciful themes of women's wear. Here, as well, once the industry had freed itself from the narrow array of applications of carded wool, the body of experience and knowledge developed in the weaving of colored wool yarns and threads was transferred to new product lines.

Gucci,
spring/summer
1999 advertising
campaign. Photo
by Mario Testino

The diverse specialties of the two districts is still clearly detectable in the range of products, a fact that is continually touted by the manufacturers. In practical terms, the specific differentiation of manufacturing methods and attitudes toward innovation that for many decades separated the industries of Prato and Biella, in terms of the simple dichotomy between woolens/women's wear" and "drapery/men's wear," continues to persist, though in different forms.

The cases of Prato and Biella are not isolated. A similar watershed—made up at once of mercantile, technical, and cultural factors—led to the production of silk in Como being directed primarily to the markets for women's wear.

In the fashion system, industrial clusters that withstand the larger currents of global competition are exceptions, and specialization in production for men or women in territorial industrial clusters is a surprising phenomenon; while it is easy to imagine the elements of rationalization and competition that go into the decision to focus a company's supply on a certain area of production, in the case of entire districts there is no single decision-making process or overriding organization that makes choices concerning the positioning of products and markets for all the companies in the area.

In the multifaceted microcosm of fashion, these phenomena make it clear that a system of companies, though small in size (as is the case in Prato and Carpi, for example), can gain enormous competitive advantages from the interrelations and ties established by proximity and by the attainment of a certain critical mass, not by the individual companies, but by the territory at large.

And on a territorial level, as well, there emerges a tendency toward the specialization of many companies, some in men's wear, others in women's wear. And for that reason the idea is becoming accepted that, in programs of development for underdeveloped areas, it is wise to operate with the idea of an industrial district in mind. This is already happening in southern Italy.

Putignano, in Puglia, manufactures bridal gowns; just a bit to the north, Andria makes men's intimate wear, while in the Salento region, on the Ionian coast, there are two districts, or clusters, specializing, respectively, in men's socks and ties. The same is true in Brolo (in Sicily), while in Lavello, a small town near Potenza, a first cooperative was founded ten years ago to manufacture women's lingerie. Today, there is a full-fledged district (50 companies, employing more than 300) producing 5 million brassieres a year (a fifth of Italy's total production). In the Sannio area, we find San Marco dei Cavoti, which specializes in the production of major items (suits, jackets) of men's wear.

The south of Italy, from this point of view, represents a sort of laboratory (very important for a discipline like economics, which encounters enormous problems when it attempts to verify the actual reactions of economic actors)

Gigli,
spring/summer
1999 advertising
campaign.
Photo by Enrique
Badulescu

facing page:
Ermenegildo
Zegna, catalogue
of the 1999/2000
fall/winter
collection.
Photo by
Mikael Jansson

that demonstrates the key role of the specialization and characterization of supply in the initial phases of economic development.

To the north, we may mention once again Castelgoffredo (near Mantua), a small town with a population of well under a hundred thousand, which produces, however, 80 percent of the women's hosiery consumed in Europe.

Globalization Reduced

Once we have studied and understood the territorial microspecializations of men's wear and women's wear manufacturing found in the industrial clusters, or districts, of Italian style, it comes as no surprise that the globalization of markets should have moved at different rates of speed, at least as far as manufacturing is concerned; more quickly in men's wear than in women's wear. The statistics of world trade offer proof.

Let us consider the countries ranking highest as world clothing exporters. If we measure their specialization in exporting men's wear or women's wear, we find that the old world, or Europe, leads in women's wear, with France coming first, and then Italy, followed by the United Kingdom and Germany, as if recapitulating the various steps in the history of the manufacture of ready-to-wear apparel.

The fact that Turkey and South Korea belong to this

group deserves comment. Turkey, an important "appendage" of the German textiles industry, has wavered for nearly all of the past century as to whether—culturally, politically, and economically—it is Europe's frontier with Asia or Asia's frontier with Europe. South Korea is unquestionably Asian, the most economically advanced of the newly industrialized Asian nations, with levels of per capita income and salaries that, until the financial collapse of 1997, were perhaps a decade behind European levels.

Among the countries specializing in men's wear, we find countries with low costs, which over the past twenty years have pursued the most aggressive politics of export penetration: China, Thailand, and Indonesia, as well as—surprise!—the United States, which is, in fact, the greatest specialist in men's wear. But what do the textiles factories of Alabama, South Carolina, and California have in common with those of Guandong in China, Sampran in Thailand, or Bandung in Indonesia? More than one might think: in the U.S. and in China, Thailand, and Indonesia, the manufacturers are largely working on a large-scale and extremely large-scale basis.

The American garment industry has chosen, programmatically, to avoid small-scale mass production, which is unpredictable and high in fashion content (a perfect identikit of the women's wear industry), and has shifted nearly all this production to the *maquiladoras*, or sweatshops, of Central America, and especially NAFTA countries, like Mexico. The American industry, therefore,

Ermenegildo Zegna

has chosen to focus on areas of manufacturing in which standardization and huge numbers, in extremely efficient and well-organized production, help to keep costs low (through economies of scale and experience) so as to compete with the huge Asian manufacturers.

This is the diametric opposite of what most of the companies in the Italian fashion system have done, where not only is the manufacturing system particularly suited to women's wear, but in general in men's wear as well the factors typical of small companies are emphasized: quality of tailoring, niche specialization, etc.

Suits and Scents

At the end of the century, however, we can begin to note clearly growing cracks in the wall that separates men's wear from women's wear. The fashion virus—a tendency to pay more attention to esthetic values than to the care of the finish, a greater sensitivity to colors and cuts than to a perfect fit—is slowly infecting the sector of men's wear. The substrates of infection are the growing acceptance of casual wear in the workplace, long dominated by tailored clothing, and a more general trend toward a greater attention to the male body, which is shaping the development of male lifestyle in recent years.

In an old Italian song, a mother is accused by her son of buying perfumes and scents only for herself. In order to take into account the growing attention to the

body and its care that seems to characterize the male of the turn of the millennium, the words to this song should be updated to include a complaint about the boy's father as well. According to a recent survey, in fact, some 48 percent of American males state that they regularly use a scent, on a daily basis. This percentage is only slightly lower than that of women (51 percent). In 1998 the sales of male perfumes in American department stores rose at twice the rate of women's perfumes (5 percent vs. 2 percent), to just under $1 billion (or 32 percent of the $3 billion in total annual sales of fragrances).

A new man, then, is moving among the counters of the department stores. He is more interested in taking care of himself and is more aware of the variety of messages he sends with his own body (and clothing): an awareness that was once the exclusive heritage of the female clientele. Attention to men's bodies is reflected as well in the boom in clothing for sports and fitness, now profoundly established in the turbulent currents of fashion, style, and luxury (soon to debut: the first line of Louis Vuitton for sports).

An Open Letter to the Men of IBM

In 1995 one of the most important temples of corporate style and formal office wear finally gave way; IBM joined the many other corporations, large and small, that have introduced dress-down days, establishing a dress-down

Salvatore Ferragamo

Friday in IBM headquarters in Armonk, New York, thus relaxing the formal dress code for employees. An event of enormous symbolic importance, this provoked an advertising campaign soon after, with a headline reading, "An open letter to the men of IBM." The ad stated: "It's welcome that IBM will relax its dress code. The men's wear industry thrives on creating clothing that allows men self-expression, personal style, and comfort. Since casual style is far from sloppy, the men of IBM and every company with relaxed dress codes will want to build new wardrobes. They will find the 'Easy Friday' collection by Bagir, dedicated to the art of dressing down." The spread of "Friday wear" along with the extension in some cases throughout the week of casual dress in the workplace has led to transformations of the market, and even to some uncertainty concerning the appropriate casual dress code, leading some American clothing manufacturers to create lines like "Corporate Casual" or "Soft Classics," with special little brochures or booklets tied to the article of clothing, explaining how to accompany and accessorize in the workplace. Casual dress, moreover, is becoming increasingly common as well in leisure situations that might once have called for jacket, trousers, shirt, and tie.

The migration of a significant share of the tailored clothing market toward casual wear, the expansion of the fashion market toward athletic apparel, and, in general, the increased fashion awareness of male consumers have had—and, above all, will have—a major impact on the

structure of the sector and on the behavior of the manufacturers. The rules and the forms of the market and the organization of the cycle of design, production, and distribution that characterize the casual wear markets have, in fact, very little in common with the same factors in the market for tailored clothing. In casual wear, for instance (as in women's wear) the phase of design involves at the same time changes in the silhouette, the models, the colors, and the fabrics, which are matched with the individual models of clothing. As in women's wear, the system of sizes is simplified. The manufacture of these products requires a lower degree of precision in the construction of the individual items, which (again, as in women's wear) can easily be delegated to independent subcontractors, both in the same country and overseas. With the changes in fashion, the range of models and style expands and contracts: more or fewer sweaters or jackets, more or fewer T-shirts, sweatshirts, or running outfits, and so forth; at the same time, the network of subcontractors used by the client companies can contract, expand, or change.

What Does it Cost to Be a Man?

In any case, as in a world turned upside down, in the male-dominated or male chauvinist society of the present day, the market for fashion continues to be dominated primarily by women's wear.

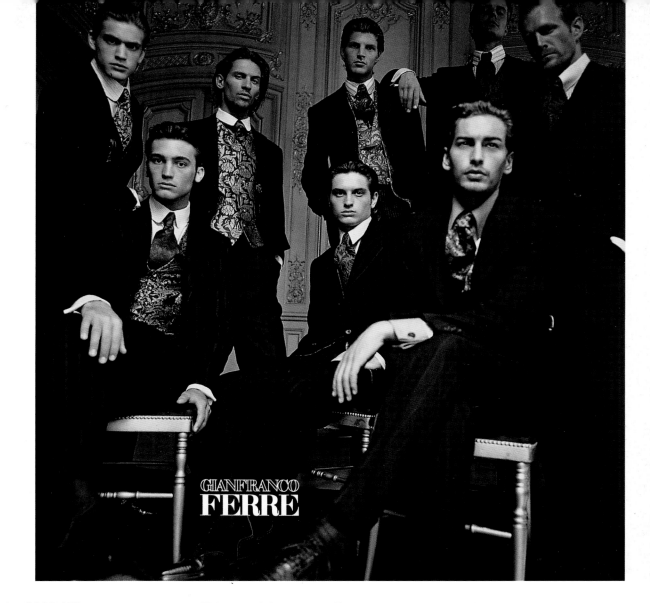

Gianfranco Ferré,
1995/96
fall/winter
advertising
campaign. Photo
by Michel Comte

facing page:
Salvatore
Ferragamo,
1999/2000
fall/winter
advertising
campaign. Photo
by Fabrizio Ferri

In the United States, out of the $238 billion spent annually by American families on clothing and accessories, only 35.7 percent (which adds up, in any case, to the considerable sum of $85 billion) is spent on men's wear products.

Only slightly larger than the American share—38 percent, equaling some $20 billion—is the share spent on men's wear in the budgets of Japanese families; this difference is largely attributable to variations in statistical categories, since the Japanese figures exclude stockings and socks and underwear, where women spend more heavily than men.

There is less precise information available concerning the European market, which in any case largely mirrors the trends found in America and Japan.

Conclusions

The juxtaposition of men's wear/women's wear represents a major factor, both of polarization and of organization, of the entire fashion system. It is central as far as trade fairs are concerned, and—in slightly more discreet roles—we find it just about everywhere: in companies, in industrial sectors, and in territorial clusters. The fact of belonging to—or producing for—one or the other half of the world population affects the economic activities, the professional choices, and the directions of development that are chosen.

This certainly has an effect on the outlooks and strategies of manufacturers: in the marketplace of the turn of the millennium, will the American model of huge corporations prevail, in which women's wear, and in any case apparel featuring an elevated level of variability, manufactured in limited numbers, is channeled through countries with low labor costs, while high-volume production, mostly intended for men, has a better chance of remaining a product of countries with high labor costs? Or is the European model, and especially the Italian model, likely to win, meaning that greater variability, unpredictability, and fashion content will correspond to a greater competitive edge that is based on the coexistence and synergy of major corporations and systems of industrial districts or clusters? The tendency at the end of the twentieth century toward a greater intensity of fashion (and therefore toward greater variability and unpredictability) in men's wear as well as women's, along with the achievements so far in the international marketplace, would encourage us to veer, in the face of an imaginary bookmaker, toward the second scenario.

In conclusion, even though television and new lifestyles are causing turmoil at the market's core, the distinction between men's wear and women's wear continues to be significant; it is no longer an overwhelming division, but it serves as a useful filter for understanding the forces that shape the apparel industry.

Antony Shugaar

THE COMEDY OF ERRORS

Gender Icons as Modular Components of Identity

Me and my brother were talking to
    each other
About what makes a man a man
Was it brain or brawn, the month you
    were born
We just couldn't understand

Our old man didn't like our appearance
He said that only women wear long hair

So me and my brother borrowed money
    from Mother
We knew what we had to do
We went downstairs, past the barber
    and gymnasium
And got our arms tattooed

Welcome to my life, tattoo, I'm a man now,
    thanks to you
I expect I'll regret you
But the skin graft man won't get you
You'll be there when I die . . .

—Tattoo, from "The Who Sell Out," 1967

Clothes aren't supposed to make the man. In fact, there is something about that smug little axiom that is profoundly subversive of the twentieth century's idea of masculinity. Earlier centuries might have allowed men to be indulgently fascinated with clothing and yet masculine. But for the past century, the idea has been that masculinity is concerned with substance and unconcerned with appearance. If clothes make the man, then what is a man? An empty suit?

Men aren't even supposed to know what makes the man. They are supposed to be men and deeply unaware of it. Men are supposed to be ignorant of clothing, even if they somehow dress well. The only true male elegance, then, would be an unconscious understanding of clothing, an instinctive selection of one look rather than another.

The song *Tattoo*—quoted on this page—dates from 1967. It is eloquent in its ironic presentation of something that looks less laughable than it once did. It was laughable at the time because a tattoo clearly represented a set of hidebound, working-class British attitudes toward masculinity. Expressed in tones of tender, almost pitying, fondness, the song attached a poetic dignity to confusion and issued a fumbling quest for clarity. To be tattooed was a semi-Neanderthal fashion statement, but it was also a singularly courageous one. "The skin graft man won't get you/You'll be there when I die" the singer declares.

Tattooing meant subscribing to an image of

Mills & Boon,
artwork for Paul
Smith,
True Brit, 1998

66

masculinity that had everything to do with nationalism, patriotism, and a narrow-minded defense of king and country. This form of machismo was male and Anglo-Saxon . . . not unlike the American equivalent, embodied in Gary Cooper and John Wayne.

Things change.

Tattoos are no longer specific signifiers of masculinity—in fact the young men of the song would probably be young women today—but they are still powerful, and increasingly popular, signifiers of identity and attitude.

The more profound a change appears to be, however, the less likely it is to be exactly what it seems.

performing other typically macho tasks, with great displays of swagger and braggadocio. Gypsy Rose Lee might have easily identified the style, if not the gender, of the well-built male construction worker who doffs his shirt for the Diet Coke break in an advertisement featuring an officeful of female executives; the women clearly consider the man little more than a sex object to be ogled from their office window.

Cowboy gear, a distinctly American apparel, fits men and women equally well. Many of the new modular styles cross ethnic and national boundaries as well. Khakis and polo shirts and the whole landed-aristocracy look once identified the British male, but it took an

The outfit that Gary Cooper wore in a movie of the Fifties—say, tight jeans, plaid shirt, bandana, sharp-toed boots—is likely to be copied identically by Marilyn Monroe in a movie of the Sixties or by Kim Basinger in a movie of the Eighties. The trope remains identical; it simply widens its field of application.

Machismo remains, but it is now modular and democratized, available to one and all. In a time when men wear scent, worry about their waistlines, and talk about their emotions; in a time when women head families, serve in the military, play basketball, and head corporations, many of the old identifying features of masculinity—such as "masculine" forms of toughness or elegance—still survive, but they are no longer limited to males.

Macho women appear regularly in Salem cigarette ads, often holding pneumatic cement hammers or

American Jew of Russian descent—Ralph Lauren—to commodify that look into something that could be worn by men, women, Brits, Yanks, and every other variation on gender, nationality, and persuasion.

As Ray Davies sang (in *Lola*), "Girls will be boys, and boys will be girls, it's a mixed-up, muddled-up, shook-up world." The mixing and shaking means that the look of the conquering Anglo-Saxon male has become a modular commodity, available to one and all—Japanese executive, Puerto Rican lesbian, Jewish professor, Sicilian college student, and so on.

The breakdown in gender distinctions seems to go hand-in-hand with the breakdown in national differences and the slow abolition of racial prejudices. Indeed, another song dating from the late Sixties points to the shallowness of equating appearance and essence. The Yardbirds sang: "Can you judge a man/By the way he wears his hair/Can you read his mind/By the clothes that he wears/Can you see a bad man/By the pattern on his tie/Well then mister you're a better man than I."

Cary Grant,
Robert Mitchum,
John Wayne

facing page:
E.S.P.A.M. School
for Hairdressers,
Milan, men's
hairstyles, world
championships in
Vienna, 1960

John Wayne on
the set of *The
Alamo*, 1959,
directed by John
Wayne. Photo by
Dennis Stock

facing page:
Marlon Brando
played Mark
Antony in the
film *Julius
Caesar*, 1953,
directed
by Joseph
L. Mankiewicz

Every once in a while the adoption of a traditionally male appurtenance by women results in something so gross and absurd that it is rejected even after the conquest of the new domain is complete—witness the "power bow," gender-crossing equivalent of the businessman's tie. The disappearance of the power bow bespeaks freedom of choice, not a resurgence of inequality.

Clearly, female equality comes replete with the freedom to adopt or reject male style, to prefer femininity to casualness or macho toughness. Women can pick and choose in what Ted Polhemus has described as "the supermarket of styles." With modular masculinity—adaptable to any and all packets of styles—comes the convenience of handy packaging and a vast assortment.

And, in keeping with the fundamental rules of modern marketing, it is not the nature of the changes that matters, it is the simple fact that there is a steady succession of changes such as to entail new reasons to buy. It is not so much the fact that men can dress like women, or women can dress like men. Both genders have been doing those things for eons. It is the fact that, having once done them, they are free to change back. In the Nineties, a new abbreviation appeared on American university campuses, to take its place alongside BMOC (big man on campus) and others: LUG (lesbian until graduation).

So what is it that divides male and female, masculine and feminine, men and women? This division may well now be optional, modular, blurry, and shifting, but it continues to exist. If in the past it was predicated on fear (of sexual deviance), duty (to procreate), and need (of various economic factors), it now is based on one primary factor: attraction.

On the matter of the dissolution of the dividing line between male and female signifiers, I have quoted extensively from pop songs of the Sixties and early Seventies. For the hard skeletal structure of the attraction and hostility between male and female, let me delve into the noir detective novel, and specifically the work of Raymond Chandler.

Chandler is strangely pertinent today. Women may wear nose rings and men may wear skirts, but the Hobbesian dynamics of sexual tension remains as it was described by Chandler. It reappears in the movies of Martin Scorsese and the Coen brothers and, more currently, the work of Neil La Bute (*The Company of Men, Your Friends and Neighbors*) or Todd Solondz (*Happiness*). It is the dark shadow that outlines and silhouettes every moment of America's enjoyment of its national wealth. It is the fundamental American artwork exported to the rest of the world.

Let one thing be clear—the lurking sense of danger and hostility that appears in Chandler's work corresponds to a very specific antagonism, not a generalized division between the sexes, but the specific tension that surrounds dating and mating, the evaluation and judgment that accompanies first meetings. And it is there, as nowhere else, that clothing matters. Husbands and wives, boyfriends and girlfriends don't judge each other by their clothing—potential couples do.

His main character, Philip Marlowe, managed to take tough American masculinity and twist it into something so alienated, so sharp, stylish, and inhuman that it turned simple detective novels into artworks as abstract and surreal as anything Picasso, Braque, and Dalí ever crafted.

Take this charming exchange between Marlowe and Vivan Sternwood, in *The Big Sleep*:

"Her voice became an icy drawl. 'Take me away from here, if you will be so kind. I'm quite sure I'd like to go home.'

"'You won't be a sister to me?'

"'If I had a razor, I'd cut your throat—just to see what ran out of it.'

"'Caterpillar blood,' I said."

In the short story, *Red Wind*, Marlowe spots a clue to a murder in the victim's knowledge of the opposite sex and its sartorial style. This knowledge is suspect, branding the victim, Waldo, as something other than an ordinary man, as a "wrong guy":

"'That's right,' I said.

"But that wasn't what I was thinking at all. I was thinking that Waldo had described the girl's clothes in a way the ordinary man wouldn't know how to describe them. Printed bolero jacket over blue crepe silk dress. I didn't even know what a bolero jacket was. And I might have said blue dress or even blue silk dress, but never blue crepe silk dress."

So he claims, but other passages from *The Little Sister* show just how well Chandler himself observed, with a sort of appalled horror, the specifics of female style:

"The bell chimed and a tall dark girl in jodhpurs opened the door. Sexy was very faint praise for her. The jodhpurs, like her hair, were coal black. She wore a white silk shirt with a scarlet scarf loose around her throat. It was not as vivid as her mouth. She held a long brown cigarette in a pair of tiny golden tweezers. The fingers holding it were more than adequately jeweled. Her black hair was parted in the middle and a line of scalp as white as snow went over the top of her head and dropped out of sight behind. Two thick braids of her shining black hair lay one on each side of her slim brown neck. Each was tied with a small scarlet bow. But it was a long time since she was a little girl."

A second passage from the same novel:

"She was wearing a white wool skirt, a burgundy silk blouse and a black velvet over-jacket with short sleeves. Her hair was a hot sunset. She wore a golden topaz bracelet and topaz earrings and a topaz dinner ring in the shape of a shield. Her fingernails matched her blouse exactly. She looked as if it would take a couple of weeks to get her dressed."

And a third:

"I looked back as I opened the door. Slim, dark and lovely and smiling. Reeking with sex. Utterly beyond the moral laws of this or any world I could imagine."

And, lest it be thought that Chandler reserves his scorn and fascination for feminine style alone, consider

this excerpt from *The Lady in the Lake*:

"Ten minutes later the same door opened again and the big shot came out with his hat on and sneered that he was going to get a hair-cut. He started off across the Chinese rug in a swinging athletic stride, made about half the distance to the door and then did a sharp cutback and came over to where I was sitting.

"'You want to see me?' he barked.

"He was about six feet two and not much of it soft. His eyes were stone gray with flecks of cold light in them. He filled a large size in smooth gray flannel with a narrow chalk stripe, and filled it elegantly. His manner said he was very tough to get along with."

For Chandler, style itself is a pact with the devil. His

James Dean in
a barbershop
in Times Square,
New York, 1955.
Photo by
Dennis Stock

character is endlessly sarcastic, witty, and alienated, but his detective hero is style-less. He has a drab little office, and his outsider status gives him a last chance at morality, at decency. In one particularly revealing passage, again from *The Little Sister*, he describes the male style that he finds "back in coptown," in the wake of a grueling all-night interrogation to which he has been subjected:

"They just sat there and looked back at me. The orange queen was clacking her typewriter. Cop talk was no more treat to her than legs to a dance director. They had the calm weathered faces of healthy men in hard condition. They had the eyes they always have, cloudy and gray like freezing water. The firm set mouth, the hard little wrinkles at the corners of the eyes, the hard hollow meaningless stare, not quite cruel and a thousand miles from kind. The dull ready-made clothes, worn without style, with a sort of contempt; the look of men who are poor and yet proud of their power, watching always for ways to make it felt, to shove it into you and twist it and grin and watch you squirm, ruthless without malice, cruel and yet not always unkind. What would you expect them to be? Civilization had no meaning for them. All they saw of it was the failures, the dirt, the dregs, the aberrations and the disgust."

These cops constitute the unchanging center of the maelstrom of style, a maelstrom of style that, for Chandler and the old masculinity of a hard-working, poorer, long-ago United States, represented a kind of corruption, a form of evil.

Masculinity and femininity persist, as solid and unbudgeable as ever. What has changed is the willingness of men and women to experiment with the outward signs of sexual identity. There is danger in the space between the sexes, but that danger can be dealt with in many ways: by accentuating or de-emphasizing gendered characteristics (such as dressing up as a sex kitten or in genderless, baggy sportswear, to name two options for women) or by adopting any of a series of archetypes (a man, for example, may choose to be a beatnik, cowboy, 1940s lounge lizard, British banker, oil-rig roustabout, and so on).

The true change, then, is that everyone is dressing up, in a playful and relatively liberated manner. This is a result of many deep changes in the United States and around the world, but of one in particular: a general rising tide of prosperity. Sharp gender distinctions have floated away on a wave of cash, and cash trumps gender every time.

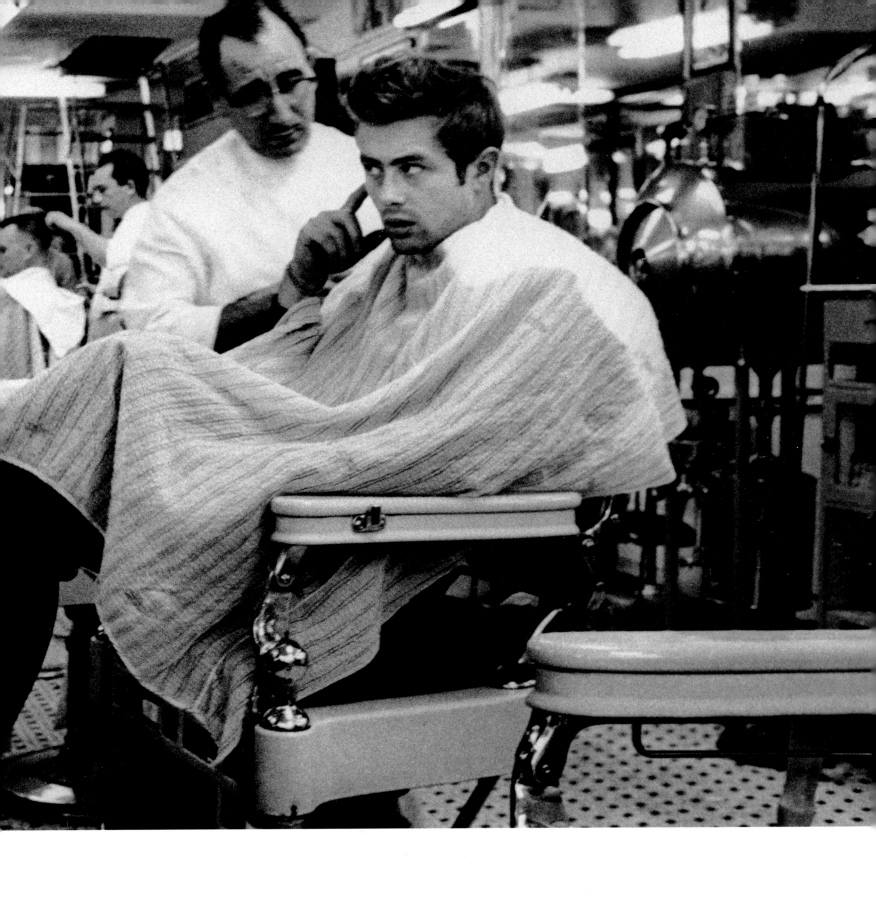

Photographs by Mark Lipson

LUCHA LIBRE

Lucha Libre,
Mexico, 1994.
Photos by
Mark Lipson

Valerie Steele

FASHIONING MEN

The Role of Fashion in the Imagination of American Men

Women are fashionable, but men are not. This, at least, is the popular opinion in America. Witness the following conversation:

"What are you writing?" asked my son.

"An article on men's fashion magazines."

"Men have fashion magazines?" he demanded in astonishment.

"Well," I hedged. "Sort of . . ."

Next to me was a stack of magazines: *Details, Esquire, Gentlemen's Quarterly, i-D, Vogue Homme, l'Uomo Vogue.* Yet, except for the two European *Vogues,* I was pretty sure that these could not really be considered fashion magazines. Admittedly, all of these publications include fashion photographs and articles on fashion. But the rhetoric on men's fashion (both within the magazines and in the wider Anglo-American culture) is based on an adamant denial that men are interested in fashion.

Men supposedly dress for comfort and function, not style. At most, they will admit that clothing can function to enhance their status and help them succeed professionally. Dress for Success is a concept that American men can understand, although it is a bit old-fashioned these days, when so-called Business Casual is the approved corporate dress code. Men's magazines do not have headlines like "The Sexiest Season in Years" or "The Fall Fashion News." Popular opinion in America holds that men, unlike women, have not been duped into

following fashion. Men who are interested in fashion are thought to be peculiar—and probably gay. Or, at least, decadent Europeans.

To the extent that some men do develop a sense of style, they are thought to derive inspiration from films, or by a process of identification with sports figures, actors or pop stars—not by looking at fashion magazines. There is certainly evidence that many men do model themselves after certain iconic masculine types. Some years ago, Richard Martin and Harold Koda organized an exhibition (and book) on men's fashion with the catchy title *Jocks and Nerds*. (In American slang, athletic young men are "jocks," while studious ones are "nerds.") Martin and Koda identified various important masculine styles, such as the athletic look, the military look, and the rebellious look. Figures such as James Dean and the young Marlon Brando epitomized the "rebel," while Cary Grant and the Duke of Windsor were prototypes of the "gentleman." These categories—and representative figures—have remained remarkably consistent over the course of the twentieth century.

The myth of the undecorated male had already begun to emerge in the middle of the eighteenth century.

Paul Smith, fall/winter 1993/1994 advertising campaign. Photo by David Bailey

Versace
Intensive,
spring/summer
1999 advertising
campaign. Photo
by Bruce Weber

facing page:
"Dark grey silver
suit, white shirt
and black leather
shoes with velcro
strap all by Boss,"
by Hugo Boss,
editorial layout
for *Arena Homme
Plus,* 1999.
Photo by
Fabien Baron

By the nineteenth century, "fashion" had become primarily associated with femininity and frivolity. In the emerging world of capitalism and political democracy, men were increasingly assumed to be serious, hardworking, disciplined citizens, so bourgeois men adopted a civil uniform consisting of dark suits and starched white shirts. Workers and soldiers were perceived as being tough, brave, and aggressive; they wore functional work clothes or uniforms. Since their physical strength was conspicuous and their masculinity incontrovertible, they were permitted more color and decoration in their clothing.

For a long time the only men's fashion magazines were professional journals for tailors. In the twentieth century, however, a few periodicals appeared for the male fashion consumer, among them *Adam: La Revue de l'Homme.* From the 1920s through the 1950s, this upscale French periodical was devoted to men's sartorial style, with an emphasis on custom tailoring and fine accessories. But with the rise of youth culture in the 1960s, old ideas about elegance and appropriate attire were increasingly discarded by both men and women. The so-called Peacock Revolution transformed men's clothing, ushering in a period of radically new male fashions—and "fashion" was the operative word, albeit briefly. Men's fashions even emphasized sexual display—tight trousers, open shirts, color, and jewelry were all flaunted. Magazines like *Playboy* eagerly promoted new styles for "swingers." By the late 1970s, however, most men had retreated to a basic wardrobe of "classics." Yet as the cultural definition of masculinity continued to evolve during the 1980s and 1990s (in response to women's changing social roles), and as the consumer society continued to expand, journalistic discourse increasingly focused on the appearance of the "New Man"—whether dressedin Calvin Klein jeans or Armani suits.

With new men came new markets, and the style press provided a guide to modern living. In his *Cultures of Consumption*, British historian Frank Mort quotes advertising executive Zed Mort, who observed in 1986: "Publishers look at women's magazines, their circulation figures and bottom line and they think: 'If we put together a road test of a new Porsche with an in-depth interview with Giorgio Armani and some stuff about personal finance, then we'll hit some sort of composite male who has all these interests.' If that were possible, it would be like finding the Holy Grail."

Dries Van Noten, fall/winter 1999/2000 advertising campaign. Photo by Tom Munro

"Jag wears overcoat by Yves Saint Laurent Rive Gauche, top by Prada Sport, jeans by Gucci, shoes by Jones Bootmaker," editorial layout, *i-D magazine,* May, 1999. Photo by Barnaby & Scott, London

The Holy Grail has proved elusive. But a survey of men's magazines does reveal important insights about how the American media talks about fashion—and what role fashion plays in American male imagery.

Fashion, for the American male, is most acceptable in the guise of a "work uniform," however this is defined. For example, in a feature entitled "Uptown Racer," *Details* combined business clothes (jacket, shirt, and tie) with trendy biker gear (leather pants by Gucci). The incorporation of biker-inspired clothing was supposed to "kick-start your business wardrobe." The status value of tailored clothing is still relatively important. American men are expected to be at least somewhat interested in the details of a tailored suit or the choice of a necktie. However, work attire, per se, is no longer masculine enough. After all, today women also work and wear tailored suits.

Fashion features therefore almost always include hyper-masculine elements. Very often the editorial strategy focuses on the creation of a "manly" image through the presentation of unequivocally "masculine" work clothes, such as blue jeans. When the clothes are given a designer edge (boot-cut jeans by Helmut Lang, $170), readers need to be reassured that they are not "fashion." Thus, for example, a fashion feature in *Esquire* stressed that "The cowboy wardrobe is a work uniform" designed for durability and versatility.

Like denim jeans, however, the clothing of the cowboy has become fashion—one of the few explicitly American fashions. Even before the development of movies like John Wayne's *The Alamo,* stories and live performances had made the cowboy an American icon. He symbolized individual freedom within the context of a mythology of the Western frontier as a place beyond the reach of modern urbanism and industrial capitalism, a world untouched by femininity and "civilization." In short, he was perfect material to be incorporated into the fashion system.

The fashion industry distinguishes different male markets, however, based on lifestyle, personality, and prestigious imitation. For example, the cowboy represents a macho he-man, the biker is a sexy rebel, and the ambitious achiever wears a sharp suit. The sex appeal associated with violence insures that variants of the military style will always come back in fashion. As the economy changes, however, we have also seen the growing importance of "geek chic." The rise of various street styles is closely associated with styles of music, such as hip hop. Masculinity, like the empire of fashion, is increasingly fragmented. Looking at American men's magazines, however, one image comes across most powerfully: the jock.

Men's magazines focus heavily on sportswear, just as the culture in general regards sports as the dominant male enthusiasm. Sporting activity not only provides license to display the male body, it also disciplines the body, emphasizing musculature—the prime visual sign of strength and virility. Editors today increasingly discuss how utility sportswear is changing men's fashion. But clothes are only part of the new fashion picture.

Whereas traditional male dress codes emphasized status and the body itself was largely concealed, the fashion discourse today emphasizes the physical strength of the male body, which is more freely exhibited in casual sports clothing. Although "fashion" is still presumed to be a frivolous subject of interest primarily to women, the body has come to be central to the idea of fashioning modern masculinity.

Dolce & Gabbana, fall/winter 1999/2000 advertising campaign. Photo by Steven Meisel

Carlo Antonelli

TONIGHT, UNDER MY TONGUE, BABY

Gender and Musical Styles

"Squeeze my lemon 'til the juice runs down my leg."
—Robert Johnson

"I want you you you you, I want to hold you be your Mother x Whore, you be my man x boy girl girl girl weirdest 2 girls in the world. We got money. Fuck you."
—Courtney Love to Kurt Cobain, in Poppy Z. Brite, *Courtney Love, The True Story*, 1999

"As wise as serpents, and as weak as lambs."
—Curtis Mayfield

Old Stuff (Still on Sale?)

The quotes that appear above (which I have in part shamelessly pilfered from the biography of Jimi Hendrix written a few years ago by Charles Shaar Murray) could serve quite adequately as the basis for a lengthy discussion of such issues as male sexuality and the idols of twentieth-century popular music or the complex interplay involved in the representation of self that is imposed by the (Super)fly's eye of the traditional mass media upon those who venture, in their salad years, as musicians or anything of the sort, to expose themselves to the most popular routine of popularity of this century: the game (happily, no longer limited to the West) of being a rock star. And the game is always the same, a yawn-

provoking mix of breaking with standard approaches, a more or less courageous exploration of the limits of common decency, and a sharp rejection of the fates (job, love, sex) of their fathers and grandfathers played by exhibitionistic individuals capable of desires (and maybe lusts) in the face of a nameless collective, sexually incompetent and prone to sudden fits of worship and adoration. Rock, then, as a survival of old rites of passage, in other words. We could even go so far as to pull into the mix good old Herbert Marcuse and Wilhelm Reich and therefore rewrite the history of pop music as a function of the shifts in equilibrium of the general axis of the male body, from rigid to oscillating, beginning with the complicated ellipses around the pelvis that gave Elvis his nickname; to the doll-like flouncing of the Beatles ("You're a bunch of sissies," as Paul's grandfather berated the Fab Four in Richard Lester's *Hard Day's Night*); the off-kilter slightly hysterical mincing steps of Mick Jagger, half dandy half macho-man; the pogo and the slashed bodies of punk; the stage diving of the penultimate generation, a progressive tangential fugue toward the greatest possible freedom of movement: ultimately, the disappearance, the absolute biodegradability of the sacred body of the rock star.

This wholesale flight from immobility can hardly help but remind us of the clearly stated observations concerning the figures—male and not male—of the eighteenth- and nineteenth-century European bildungsroman and the

temporal experiment that the protagonists of those books undertake in order to flee from maturity, inevitably seen as a loss, a stiffening, the end of life. Instead, they seek to seize every opportunity to have "experiences," to quest for intensity or, better yet, authenticity, the bright flame of real life. Betraying tradition, then, is equivalent to attaining success, or else (as Honoré de Balzac suggests with Lucien de Rubempré in *Lost Illusions*) to the way the mechanisms of fashion work in book publishing (later, in music publishing): one is discovered, one is launched on the market, one becomes a hit, one becomes a familiar name, one falls from public awareness, one is discarded

entirely. How many teenage pop idols in the past fifty years have experienced this nineteenth-century misfortune? Still, we cannot help but think of postwar "pop rock" as the only true "education novel" for millions of teenagers around the world in the last few decades, with all the minidramas that we mentioned. It is no accident, after all, that Elvis rises up, unrivaled, dominating the landscape. First as an expression of savage and uncontaminated beauty (Elvis, prettier than the women in his movies, Elvis censured on the *Ed Sullivan Show* in 1956, shown only from the waist up so as not to show his enraged, flamboyant pelvis, etc.); and then Elvis, wasted, out of breath, dazed in a

Lenny Kravitz.
Photo by
Harry Bordem

seem more like a bunch of dear old friends that got tangled up in horribly complicated problems than they seem like scintillating role models.

Unless we take into consideration this central interplay of mirrors and glances, this public pillorying of the fragility of the star and his body (male, in this case), we can't fully appreciate the variations that have emerged in the last few years, and we will thus continue to find interesting the presumed exaltation of the authentic sensuality of black stars ("I got my mojo working," and all that); the unsuccessful efforts to imitate the same in the gesticulations of the "white negro" (so dear to the Beats but also to white B-boys of recent years); the tired carny freak shows and the use of makeup in the endless masochism of hard rock; or, worse still, the gender tourism (to use a term coined by Simon Reynolds and Joy Press) between male and female in the now three-decades-old game of androgyny played by certain stars. Moreover, we will be unable to applaud and appreciate the laudable efforts of certain contemporary males to escape these grim destinies.

The Hypermarket of Frozen Role Models

As in an adult comic book or in a cyberpunk or splatterpunk short story (with their twofold ties of blood to pop music, evident from the very root), at a certain point the wax museum of rock appeared to certain kids as an interesting warehouse of second hand costumes, an abandoned atelier. For at least the entire Eighties, there was talk of a postmodern sensibility (though by that time that particular school of thought already had at least twenty candles on its birthday cake), and then it became increasingly clear that the apparent weakness of the attitude actually concealed a surprising awareness of the personal risks involved.

On the one hand, there are the interesting sexual and stylistic nuances, substrates of an unashamed artificiality, that emerged from the previous two decades, with the great forerunner Brian Ferry, with Brian Eno and Roxy Music, and then the Human League, Spandau Ballet, Wham (culminating splendidly in the solo outing of George Michael), Duran Duran, Boy George and Culture Club, Frankie Goes to Hollywood, Marc Almond and Soft Cell, right up to the Pet Shop Boys, New Order, The Smiths, and Morrisey (who from the beginning told any journalist who would listen that he hadn't had sex for centuries).

worldwide telecast in 1973; and then in 1977 finally killed by a general overdose of pharmaceuticals, a potpourri of controlled substances and alcohol. A perfect beginning (marked by a sharp social climb, talent winning out and rising from the very bottom of society) and a deplorable end. A warning to everyone. And it is no accident, for that matter, that his name tops the list of a recent survey done by *Time* magazine among its readers on the most important men of the century. The living-dead phantom of Elvis (the "Dead Elvis" of Greil Marcus's essay by that name) does more than fill the pages of American tabloids; he emerges, a nightmare figure with all that sequined bric-a-brac that he would wear in his desperate later years, in the sleepless night of any self-respecting male music star. No one better than Warhol understood his perfectly contemporary tragic stature: "In the figures of Elvis, Liz, Michael, Oprah, Geraldo, Brando and the like we witness … the general humiliation of the public body. The bodies of these public figures are prostheses for our own mutant desirability" (quoted by Hal Foster in his essay on Warhol, "Death in America"). And, for that matter, wasn't Warhol shot, just like Lennon? He, too, was torn to pieces by his own public image. More than inspiring admiration or envy, with the passing of time, in this year with three zeroes and none of those old numbers, the figures of Elvis, Andy, Jimi, John, Kurt, et al., inspire more pity than lust; they

On the other hand, in the Nineties, we find the self-consciously dramatic life experiences (no less romantic, and Romantic, in the nineteenth-century sense of the term, smelling, therefore, like teen spirit) of Nirvana and grunge in general or, say, Nick Cave, the enchantingly cu-u-u-ute vulnerability of Billy Corgan and Smashing Pumpkins, or the more disrespectful vulnerability of Trent Reznor and Nine Inch Nails, the heroin/surf style of Perry Farrell and Jane's Addiction, the tattooed biceps of Henry Rollins, and the overweening references-to-the-past of Oasis and Blur (with plenty of "good guys vs. bad guys" Sixties byplay, striped sweaters, parkas, and Lambrettas, but helicopters, too), Stone Roses, Primal Scream, Manic Street Preachers, Pulp, Verve (for their second video, they had the nerve to show off the new loft they had just purchased in the Docklands with the money from their first video), Prodigy, Placebo, Suede, and Gay Dad. Or the splendid parody of Hendrix, but done somewhere midway between *Playgirl* and *Vogue*, by Lenny Kravitz, himself a veritable playmate of the previous decade. "In the late Eighties and the Nineties," writes Neil Tennant of the Pet Shop Boys in his introduction to the catalogue of the "Icons of Pop" exhibition at the National Portrait Gallery in London, "the apparently iconic visual statements could probably be read as ironic. The past is always with us. Every generation finds its own way of dealing with Fury's (or Elvis's) gold lamé suit or Keith Richards' black mascara or punk cut-up fashion and slogans." The important thing is to fish out only the most amusing things. The style of pop star in the last few years is intrinsically an awareness of playing with complex and stratified cultural codes involving the body and the public image. People are widely aware of this, even twenty-year-olds. It is in this divide that the new male icons in music present interesting variations on those of the past. As if the general swan song of flexibility and temporary jobs had rendered temporary and flexible (and, therefore, a genuine job, or perhaps, a McJob) the intellectual labor of pop, and therefore closer to the fears and the strange opportunities of our everyday life as doubt-ridden males.

The hundreds of thousands of pseudostars abandoned in the street of failure to lick their wounds must have served some purpose. If nothing else, they helped us to understand that, real disasters aside, in an average life span of eighty years, you might even become a rock star for a certain period of time (take it from the forefathers, Andy and Bowie), but then you might do something else, you might have children, you might tend bar in the tropics, you might found a software company, you might actually try to do something genuinely experimental, you might become a monk. In the awareness of the infinite multidimensionality of single identity, of the strange consistency of the contemporary persona, of the performative character (to borrow a phrase from Judith Butler) of one's own sexual gender, becoming a male role model as a pop star is, in the final analysis, just one of those accidents.

Musicals of Old Rock, and, How Could We Forget, the Problem of the Voice

Of course, there is Jagger as an alternative example, showing that it is possible to be sixty years old, at once puppet and puppet master of one's own masculine public image. Or else, Bon Jovi or even Bruce Springsteen, pretending to be the same, unchanged, a millionaire dressed in work clothes (as Simon Frith once nicely pointed out), partying with his old high school buddies, with a perfect white T-shirt and a pair of jeans that are always tight, front and back (though a girlfriend of mine says that the golden age is over, and that the ideal vintage for Springsteen's cute butt was 1984-85). Or like Michael Jackson (about whose priceless role as a cartoonish mutant inside Black culture much has already been written) or Aerosmith or Kiss or (if they still exist) Guns 'n' Roses, in a funnier way, punching the air or thrusting their pelvises—ah, we remember as if it were yesterday. Clearly, for one and all the spectacle of rock (and allied industries) is stuff to be categorized with *Les Misérables* or *Cats* (if not with *Hair*, Broadway for hippies), however much we may sincerely love musicals. The rock star knows that the myth of authenticity is a laughable thing when performed in front of tens of thousands of people, and he is trying to make his audience aware of it. For that matter, what smattering of authenticity can survive in studio recordings, the tracks from CDs that the audience in stadiums demands to hear reproduced verbatim in live performances, what can be considered authentic except for the profoundly moving spectacle of the fans themselves?

facing page:
Andy Warhol.
Photo by
Bruce Davidson

Mr. Eliminator,
Dick Dale and his
Del-Tones, 1964,
Capitol Records

Windowlicker,
Aphextwin, 1999,
Warp Records

88

Liberace,
American pianist
and singer.
Photo by
Philippe Halsman

Or perhaps there is nothing left but the famous "voice" so touted by Roland Barthes (and we have to go back to Barthes and his *Mythologies* every time that we wish to examine a mass phenomenon of the last century), the voice that carries the singer's entire body with it. "How did this century begin?," writes Ian Penman in a recent issue of *The Wire*. "Listening. A middle-aged bourgeois psychoanalyst in Vienna takes the time to listen, that's all, and it blows our world apart.... Microphonics and psychoanalysis—these new phantom sciences—make tremors speak from the invisible inside, where we can neither see nor want the very thing we have always been scared to have revealed. Other voices. New grammatologies of analysis and amplification. The microphonic song insinuates encoded bodily truths in a code often so subtle as to be almost inaudible . . . From now on, song will be an ethereal, porous space in which voices lose their demarcation, in which the ordinary is made uncanny."

Welcome, then, to the castle of mirrors of pop. In the face of fifty-seven TV channels (and nothing on, as Bruce says), Bowie/Ziggy Stardust (the unrivaled icon of the cross-dressing and more-or-less political androgyny of the time, along with the falsettos of disco music and the farcical operatic drag-shows of Freddy Mercury and Queen) glimpses Elvis's ghost in Nicolas Roeg's *The Man Who Fell to Earth*, and shouts: "Go away, leave me alone!" Some amusement park of success, some Velvet Goldmine.

Nostalgia and Exoticism of the Golden Years (of Pop)

Forget about eyeliner, guitar riffs, and fireworks. This may be why, for the first time, the current generation of twenty- and thirty-year-olds prefers the music of their grandfathers to the rock of their uncles and the punk of their older brothers. Music by/for ghosts and phantoms, music that creates fantastic distortions and errors of perception (see David Toop, *Exotica*). And the heart-on-the-sleeve martini-in-hand romanticism of the crooners of the Fifties and Sixties, bachelors worthy of Jack Lemmon in Billy Wilder's *The Apartment* (or Marlon Brando and Frank Sinatra, mama's boy, in Herman Mankiewicz's strange musical, *Guys and Dolls*), or later on smarmy operators like Serge Gainsbourg or Lee Hazlewood, all so indecisive and two-dimensional, so subtle and bombastic, all seem like the most serious portrayal of masculine fragility (and its delicate sentimentality) rather than the clean-scrubbed little faces (and perfectly designed at a drawing-board, if you read the CBS press releases of the time) of the "authentic" Dylan of a few years later. Or, for that matter, of Iggy Pop with his cock in his hand in *Raw Power*, not to mention Marilyn Manson's old suburban game of scaring the neighbors, without even that hint of Burtonian tenderness of an Edward Scissorhands (if a pair of new tits were all that was needed to overcome the end of patriarchy, then we would all have solved these problems a while ago).

Phantoms and ghosts, we were saying. What does this have to do with the heavy-handed colonialism imposed by Anglo-Saxon pop rock (and by the quasi-military entertainment industry that produced it) on the tender young consciousnesses of the entire planet? On the one hand, we find a spectral Presley with tight trousers behind the cardboard backdrops of Acapulco or Hawaii or else a hologrammed Michael Jackson in Shanghai or a grinning Bono in Mexico City. On the other hand, in perfect counterpoint, we see the current nostalgia for "real" male romanticism in the little old Cubans excavated by Ry Cooder in the *Buena Vista Social Club*, shot by Wim Wenders for the film of that name, perhaps the true models of masculinity at the turn of the millennium. Or else the Malian musician Ali Farka Touré, or the late and lamented Nusrat Fateh Ali Khan and Fela Kuti, the latter even better in the Puerto Rican remix of the Masters at Work. Or the complex modernist solutions of Brazilian tropicalismo, with the lovely Caetano Veloso leading the pack. The Other, and it is an Elderly Other, has been among us for some time. The Other is also a ghost, and phantom, and fantasy, just as we are for him. Not so much because of the commercialization of world music, undertaken at times recklessly over the past twenty years (certainly creating interesting juxtapositions between differing models of masculinity, but no more so than those recounted in the diaries of an ethnographer written, his heart on his sleeve, by Michel Leiris, a good seventy years previous), as much as because of the definitive collapse of the Eurocentric model, to make way for a worldwide dispersal of places of origin of the stars and their imitators.

If we look at the little magazines for Filipina girls that we find on the newsstands in polyglot cities around the world, we cannot help but be amazed at the strange involuntary parodies of Western boy-bands created by partially naked young men wearing underpants from their local open-air market in place of designer skivvies by Calvin Klein, part Chicano, part Asian, part Yankee, as if to say, the perfect population of the coming century. "Filipinos are the ultimate outsiders: hybrid and resilient masters of eerie mimicry and witty appropriation. We are tropical chameleons, elegant dancers, and funky, soulful musicians.

Hiro-Kun, winner of the virtual dance contest *Bust-A-Groove*, Sony Playstation, 1999

Robbie Williams

It's not for nothing that the best bands in Asia—the ones who can segue smoothly from perfect covers of Prince's naughty *Kiss* to Debbie Boone's super-schmaltzy *You Light Up My Life*—are Filipino," points out Jessica Hagedorn in her essay, "Music for Gangsters and (Other) Chameleons," in *Stars Don't Stand Still in the Sky*. Among the transnational connections underway, this is only one of the stories of shattering dominant cultural codes (and the successful model of masculinity linked to them) that we can find scattered everywhere.

Think of the loony depiction of male eroticism on the covers of cassettes and video clips of Arab or South American pop (and the ambiguous Ricky Martin represents nothing more than the tip of the iceberg), with unlimited colonial distortion in case of success, as in the case of Khaled and the African stars of Paris in the Eighties. The Eurocentric fascination with the mistakes of modernity is the counterpart: there are plenty of fanzines and magazines on odd Kazakh versions of R 'n' R, glittering Indian teenage pop, punky ex-Yugoslavian turbofolk, strange noise-driven Japanese hard rock. How many models of difference does all this stuff bring to our lives?

A Relaxed (and Perhaps Equally Sexy) Anonymity

"And yet, only slowly are scholars beginning to realize that the musics and audiences that constitute popular music are much more diverse and multiple than we have been willing to admit (including, even in the U.S., Indian film music, Vietnamese pop music, Vegas pop, and Broadway musicals)," writes Lawrence Grossberg in an essay entitled "Same As It Ever Was? Rock Culture. Same As It Ever Was! Rock Theory," in *Stars Don't Stand Still in the Sky*. "Moreover, such work is only now beginning to confront the limitations of using communicative models to study such mass phenomena. Such models isolate texts from audiences and contexts and then struggle to reconstitute the relationship through notions of expression, signification, and representation. But popular music is

so deeply and complexly interwoven into the everyday lives of its fans and listeners that its study, even more than that of other cultural forms, has to recognize that the music is inseparable from the entire range of activities that fill up our lives, activities that are defined by and respond to the contrary, sometimes terrifying, and often boring demands of work (paid and unpaid, domestic and nondomestic), education, politics, taxes, illness, romance, and leisure (whether sought out or enforced)."

Overshadowed by the suddenly and newly sexy "older man" (who was certainly already richer) and by the division of the planetary waters and air, shrunken by the well established presence of strong female role models in the sphere of international pop (a complex and major topic, which we shall address elsewhere), weakened by their awareness of the precarious nature of musical labor, tired of doing their shopping in the supermarket (actually the hypermarket) of styles, a number of new male figures in world pop have slowly altered their strategies. One factor, of course, is technology and the possibility, widely noted, of making music in your own bedroom, putting it online (even the music of twelve-inch vinyl recordings has been put online, and there it remains), and creating worldwide hits. Another factor is the widespread awareness that pop music is part of the basic tissue of everyday life, bringing with it not only icons that can be printed on T-shirts, but such common feelings as corporeal impulses (and corporeal weariness), such as emotional ties, identity, energy, pleasure (and the shadows of pleasure). The DJ stars of contemporary pop (Norman Cook alias Fat Boy Slim, Howie B, Chemical Brothers, Leftfield, U.N.K.L.E., Orbital, Underworld, and even Massive Attack) seem to bring a greater awareness of these changes, and difficulties of finding a normality to accommodate this realization.

With procedures similar to those used in much contemporary art, with its taste for the complexity and density of the everyday (found in recent years in fashion images in such magazines as *Purple, Self Service, Big, Surface,* etc.), they appear as thirty-year-old males, with notable bags under their eyes, far from any lamé glamour, however reference-oriented, and also far from the lost Romantic warriors of the past, guys you could ask about their car insurance and how much they pay. They don't appear in videos, or if they do, their image is so normal that it verges on insignificant. They dress in chic and mysterious casualwear, or technical clothing that could be worn anywhere, in any context, just like their colleagues of the same age in the immaterial service industries of the world. Perhaps they have children, and are thus parents though children themselves. They are glad to work on obscure projects, for little money, and at the same time they enjoy an odd and transitory moment of stardom. They work on numerous fronts because they know that sooner

or later everything will change for them, and they deal with everyday life with a strange, open, and curious attitude, far removed from the Iron John of Robert Bly and far closer to the issues of the bulletin of English male self-awareness, *Achilles Heel* (among the latest subjects covered, "Men & Sports," "Men & Health," "Men & Fear," "Man & Work," "Men & Fatherhood").

The techno scene and related scenes of the past fifteen years, especially in Germany and the rest of northern Europe, characterized by the quest, sometimes an obsessive quest, for anonymity behind abstract abbreviations and initials and the creation of a diffuse, plural, sexually expansive subject rather than monadic singularities, has certainly created a generation that is more aware of changes in the common space and that, with the passage of time (most of the DJs are now middle-aged men, by this point), has generated an idea of masculinity that is closer to the hardships and traumas that make up the lives of most people ("Gay eroticism has filtered, via house and techno, into the body-consciousness of straight, working class boys," points out once again Simon Reynolds in *The Sex Revolts*). But even outside of

the latter sphere, there are noteworthy phenomena: from the biotech anonymity of male pop groups from some battle of the bands, normal neighborhood street kids (full-fledged male impersonators, forced to subject their interchangeable bodies to the desirous gaze of men and women, and in this context quite close to the circulating serial nature of the male bodies persecuted by the fear of being insignificant, products of twenty years of work on the part of the style industry, from Nick Kamen's 1985 Levi's commercial on), to the strange cosmetic creation, entirely superhuman and smooth, composed of titanium and moisturizing cream, of the Black male (and young Black female) cousins of R 'n' B all the way out to the apparently expressionless style—smacking of intelligent nerd—of Beck and the school of isolationist post-rock (with a debt to the chic normality of their forerunners, R.E.M.).

And then there is the remarkable work on identity of the English genius of electronics, Aphextwin, who—in the videoclip (directed by Chris Cunningham) and the cover of his single *Windowlicker*—is transformed into a multiple lapdancer with bikini underpants and beard. Which is not to leave out the normal (but eminently slappable) faces of the Beastie Boys, the survivors of Everlast, or even the Fun Loving Criminals or the historic Faith No More. Or the pitch darkness in which the second-generation Caribbean Tricky surrounds his public image during his live concerts, in the absolute absence (which is extremely potent in erotic terms) of the colonial styles present in the "sex-machine" sexuality exhibited by Tricky's musical forefathers, with the single deeply moving exception of Marvin "Trouble Man" Gaye (and, alternatively, by the science-fiction carnival sideshow of George Clinton and, in part, Prince, Sly Stone, Miles Davis, Sun Ra and his various astropartners, or such scientists of dub as Lee Perry).

It is within these interstitial spaces that we can find representations of masculine sensibility that are better suited to the times, certainly not in the reigning parody of the androgynous or the mutant, or the terrifying product of "profound masculinity" (in pop music as well) given by the linkage among the sadomaso style of certain gay males, the sensitive style of the new men in glossy magazines for men, and the masochistic fantasies of being an eternal victim, as expressed by Stallone or Metallica (as David Savran rightly points out in his recent book, *Taking It Like a Man*). The new century, then, begins for new (and old) men with a series of figures that become more fragile and vulnerable as they become more muscular (distant, then, from the uterine regression of certain soft and pastoral figures of the past), serpents and lambs at the same time, like in the wonderful video of *Scar Tissue* by the Red Hot Chili Peppers: four bodies, four surfers, consumed, wasted, and yet perfectly fit, topped by faces of thirty-year-olds who have been prematurely aged by desires and doubts (the latter, at least, legitimate), by the difficulties of staying on their feet, and yet still together, after a night of partying with friends, licking their wounds as it occurs to them, singing old and new songs, lounging in an old convertible, driving at a moderate speed in a desert, just any old desert, toward the rising sun. And still, pretty sexy, no?

The Village
People

overleaf:
Elvis
Impersonators,
Las Vegas, 1998.
Photo by
John Londei,
London

91

Anna Lombardi

SEX OBJECTS

Portrait of a Real Man

Real Man has a powerful car. At least, a sports car. Or at the very least, a big car. At least, a car with a few extra options. At least, a black car. Real Man has a motorcycle. Or at least a scooter. Or a bicycle. Nowadays, they even make bicycles with motors, so, fatties, there is a future for you as well. The best is a street bike with a large-displacement engine. If Real Man is sporty, then he has a dirt bike, which he carefully garages in the winter. If he is more refined, he has an antique bike, but then he is not really a Real Man: he is eccentric.

Real Man is athletic. Tennis rackets, golf clubs. Slingshots and archery bows. Perhaps Real Man plays squash, or perhaps he buys a punching bag and boxing gloves, and works out at home with them; if he is young at heart, then he owns a pair of rollerblades, complete with kneepads and elbow pads and a helmet. And if he is a Super Real Man, then there are extreme sports: let the skies split asunder: base jumping, bungee jumping, and skydiving, as well as paragliding and hang gliding. Let the waters part: rafting, hydrospeed, and kayaking. Then there are boats: sailboats or speedboats, depending on the muscular level. If our Real Man has too big a gut to be welcome at a fitness club, he may have a rowing machine by his bed. Last, if he has no muscles at all, because he is lazy, perhaps he just dreams about

adventure travel and buys athletic gadgets of every sort (from key rings to soccer balls) with the names of his favorite teams, for himself and for his son, or else he just watches a lot of sports on television. He may play chess, if he was educated in the English manner.

Real Man hunts. He hunts animals and he hunts women. Therefore, he has a rifle in his closet and a pistol in his top drawer. He loves knives, even kitchen knives. Objects with a phallic shape, say the experts. Then he loves the sax and the trumpet, not to mention the trombone, and, of course, pool cues and fishing poles. And pens: what a memorable gesture it is to pull a fountain pen out of your breast pocket and draw attention with a special ink; an intellectual pencil or a truly remarkable ballpoint pen will produce the same effect. Likewise, the car, the motorcycle, and every other sort of thing that Real Man likes to surround himself with are pure extensions of the phallus. Technology heightens his performance, and so he indulges in a passion for microscopes, telescopes, still cameras,

Giuseppe
Di Stefano in
his Ferrari

Philips Cool Skin
razor, HQ 563,
1999

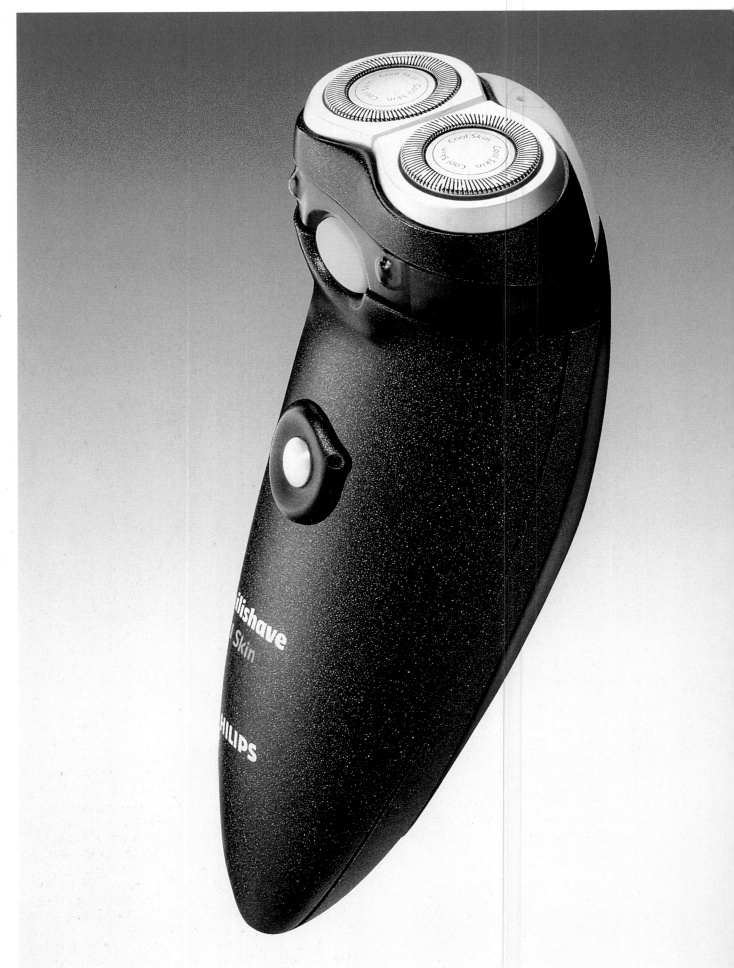

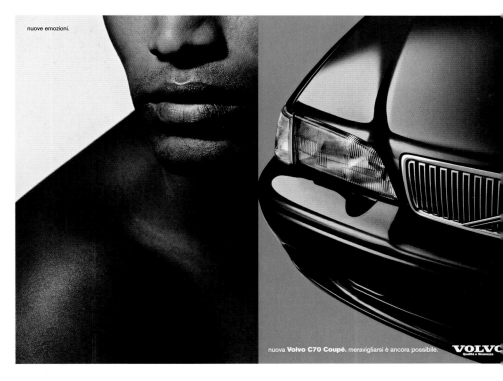

and video cameras; the most powerful stereos, the most up-to-date computers, the biggest-screen television sets, and the latest-model cell phones. Power tools and other equipment have the same effect, and perhaps that explains his woodworking set, his interest in fixing cars, his dabbling in chemistry—all adult pastimes. The ultimate explanation seems to be an animal instinct for self-preservation. Best wishes for sons, not daughters.

In the remote and unlikely case that Real Man is actually a stay-at-home, a homebody, like most of our super-endowed daredevils, then he enjoys modelmaking, building little airplanes that nobody will ever pilot, motorcycles and cars that he can never drive out of a showroom. If he is having a second childhood, electric trains and train sets are his thing. If he has no rifle of his own, then he may spend his time painting the rifles of tiny toy soldiers that he can march off to imaginary

wars. If he is well read, then he will reproduce exact and stationary strategies of real wars, taken from precise accounts found only in special books, for men only.

I have heard accounts of Real Man in the kitchen, but I have more than my share of doubts; maybe one in a hundred thousand. There are the famous chefs, but they hardly count. What would count would be a Real Man who cooks twice a day, and does the shopping to boot. Where is *that* Real Man? The domestic environment is relegated to wives or, in wealthier neighborhoods, to housekeepers. What is spreading at an amazing pace is *Homo technologicus,* who also limits his activity to the domestic front, but who is lost in a virtual world; hence the statistics on the diminution of desire, growing impotence, and the boom in sales of Viagra. People say: he is just sensitive! I say he is scared. He dreams of great conquests.

When he goes out in search of women, our Real Man doesn't mind frequenting prostitutes; after all, he

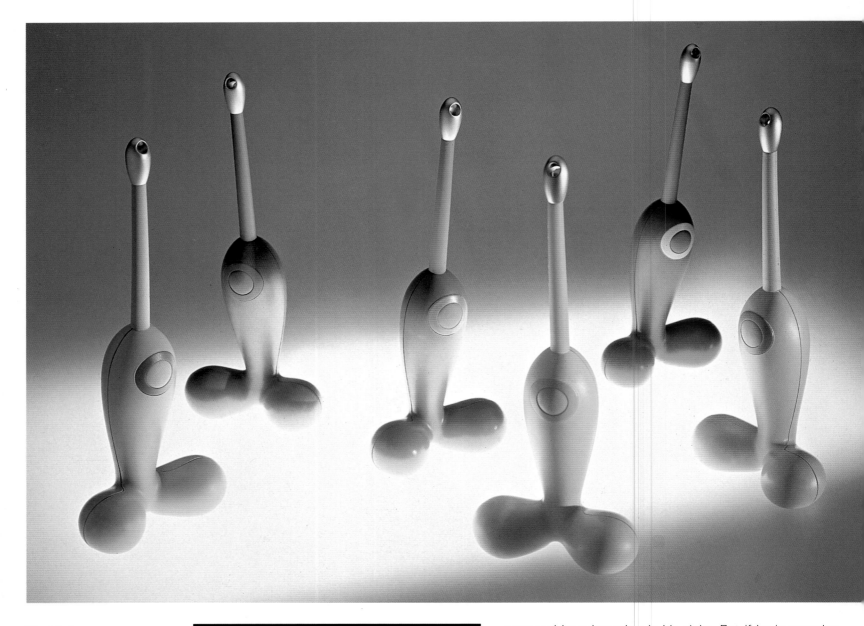

Firebird,
design by
Guido Venturini
for Alessi, 1993

Model of
a skyscraper,
Green Bird, 1996

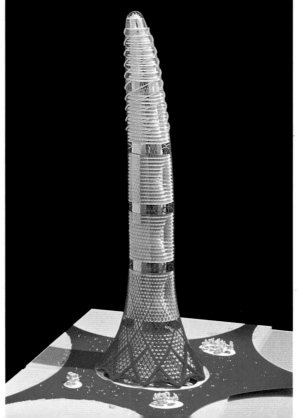

pays and he takes what is his right. But if he is pursuing the woman of his dreams, or at least a woman with whom he wants to prove to himself just what a man he really is, then he knows that he must be ready and well prepared to win out over all potential rivals and adversaries. And that is when the array of products and possessions mentioned above truly comes in useful. Like a pigeon puffing itself up, he revs up his motorcycle, or else he twists his neck around, flashing his sunglasses from the window of his powerful car, and then screeches off from a standing start. Or else he shoots his cuffs and takes a look at his wristwatch: another memorable gesture. It would appear that people are waiting for him somewhere. Instead, he is simply showing off how much money and how much power he has, how athletic and therefore how healthy he is, how refined and just how superior he feels. Perfect for the propagation of the species. Real Man. And just where is he going in such a hurry? Home, to fry up some eggs; or to a restaurant to have a salad; or to his mother's house to eat something; or home to his wife and children, where he smooths his feathers and slips into a pair of domestic slippers.

Twelve-volt
Firestorm
KC1282CK
battery-powered
drill, Black &
Decker

Thomas Hine

MICKEY ROONEY AND THE DOWNSIZING OF MAN

Male Discontent in the Society of the Spectacle

A great man is only the reflection of a great boy in a larger mirror.

—Spoken to actor Mickey Rooney by Ann Shoemaker, the actress playing his mother in *Strike Up the Band* (1940)

Even in 1940, it was unlikely that movie audiences believed that Mickey Rooney, then twenty years old, would grow up to be a great man. He was, at the time, one of Hollywood's biggest stars. One secret to his allure was that it seemed he would never grow up at all.

Even so, this nugget of ersatz maternal wisdom contained an idea that has since reverberated through the decades. Mickey Rooney represents a milestone in the development—or perhaps degeneration—of American manhood. Audiences of 1940 would have imagined the youth looking into the mirror to see the man he would become. Now, sixty years later, middle-aged American men—even the president himself—look in the mirror and see a boy who has been magnified perhaps, but never entirely finished. American men have a real problem feeling, and thus looking, grown up.

Rooney made fifteen movies playing the role of Andy Hardy, a confident, charming, and relentlessly peppy young man who inhabited a comfortable suburban world filled with big houses, mature trees, and MGM starlets. He was the mischievous, hyperactive offspring of a respected judge, portrayed by the granitic Lewis Stone. Judge Hardy was a wise, sometimes stern, and ultimately kindly and loving father. The relationship between father and son represented an ideal of American middle-class family life. Nevertheless, an enormous generation gap yawned between the two of them, one that existed not so much in the script as in the very nature of the two actors. Nobody viewing the film could possibly imagine that Andy Hardy would ever grow up to be a man remotely like his father. He seemed to be a different kind of creature entirely, one who could never hope to acquire the patina of age and authority that virtually defined the character of the judge. Indeed, when we look at photographs from the early twentieth century or earlier, American men at the age of twenty appear to be fully mature men. Alexis de Tocqueville, who visited the U.S. during the 1830s, was struck by the early age at which American boys were accepted and respected as fully competent men. But during the last half century, twenty-year-olds have come to seem younger and younger in their appearance, and so have thirty-, forty-, and fifty-year-olds. (There comes a point, though, as

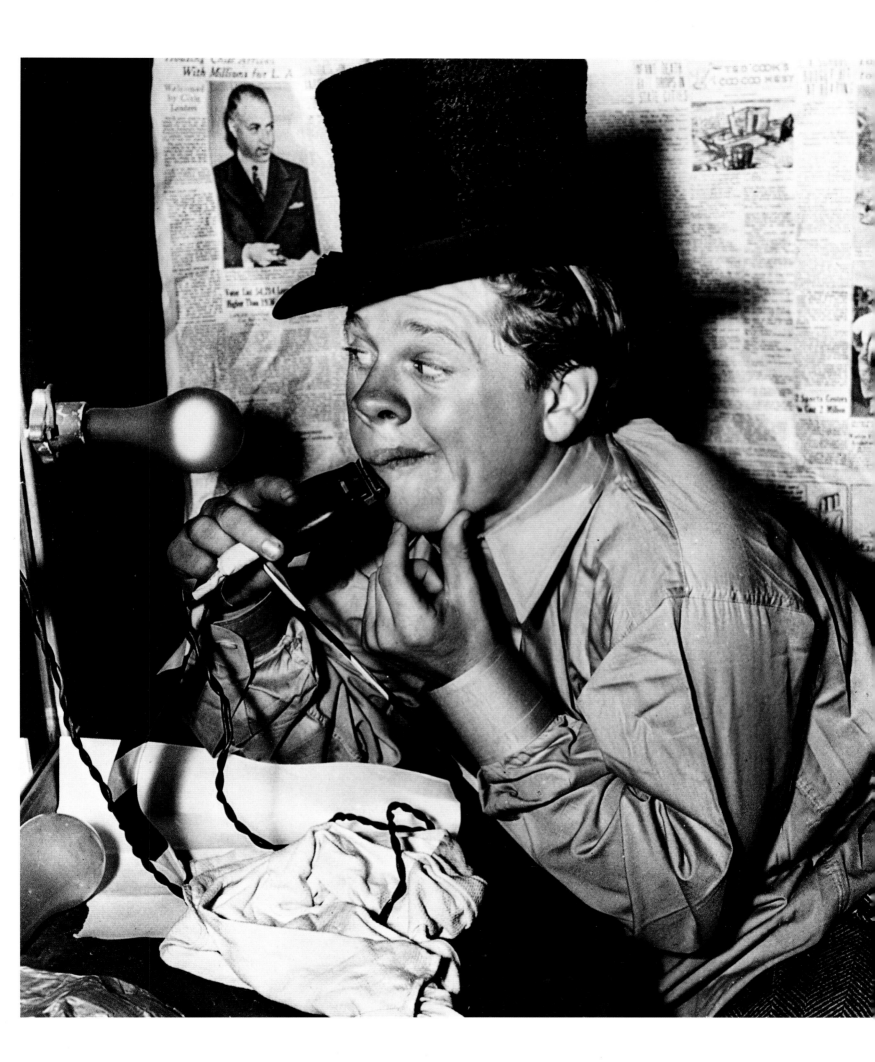

preceding page:
Mickey Rooney
shaving during
a break in the
filming of *Young
Tom Edison*,
1940, directed by
Norman Taurog

Rooney's example demonstrates, when youthfulness does disappear, to be replaced not by confident maturity, but by physical decay.)

Examples of this phenomenon abound in public life. Senator Albert Gore, for example, was a classic Judge Hardy type, a Washington monument who, like many politicians of his era, wore his hair in a great white mane that served as an emblem of experience and power. His son, Vice President Albert Gore—you can call him Al—might have been more comfortable in this bygone age. He is required, however, to be younger and looser, and to poke fun at his own seriousness by dancing a very wooden macarena.

This unwillingness to appear grown up is not a product of better nutrition and medical care, or age-defying skin preparations. It is more a matter of attitude and expectations. Earlier in the century, young American men were far more likely to live with their families, but they sought to project an image of maturity. Now, a computer billionaire is perfectly satisfied to appear as a work in progress. It was once possible for American men to aspire to a mature and stable identity, rooted in a lifelong occupation, a stable community, an enduring marriage. Now, especially in the occupational realm, we have to learn to live amid constant disruption. Like the characters Rooney played, we're scrambling to put on a show.

I'm not trying to argue that Rooney was the cause of any preconceived notions, merely that he was an early symptom of a shrunken conception of adulthood that has become ever more evident in recent years. Rooney, the child of show business parents, was an ambiguous figure from the beginning, making his movie debut at the age of six playing a cigar-smoking midget. Later, he spent twenty years playing characters in their teens, and he was nearly forty when he finally left juvenile roles behind. Moviegoers were aware of a mismatch between his on-screen ingenuousness and off-screen experience. In 1942, for example, the year he made *The Courtship of Andy Hardy*, Rooney married the first of his eight wives, the sex goddess Ava Gardner.

Even when he was in his teens, Rooney suggested competence and ambition beyond his years. The plot of many of his films, including *Strike Up the Band*, hinged on Mickey proving that young people could perform far better than adults gave them credit for. Yet, especially in the Andy Hardy films, Rooney embodied an emerging conception of life's stages. He was the exemplar of a new kind of figure that got its name the year he turned twenty-one: the teenager.

The teenager is such a familiar, and seemingly real, figure in world culture that it is surprising how recently the label emerged. It happened by accident, mostly as a by-product of the worldwide economic crash that began in 1929. Among the millions of suddenly unemployed masses were large numbers of workers in their teens. Those who had managed to hold on to their jobs during the early Depression had a rude

this page and facing page: Mickey Rooney with Judy Garland in a scene from the film *Andy Hardy Meets Debutante* 1940, directed by George B. Seitz

awakening in 1933, when President Franklin D. Roosevelt—a grown-up if ever there was one—instituted a program that forced companies to fire the young, the unmarried, and women, and to replace them with the older male breadwinners.

While some worried that this policy would drive young people to revolutionary barricades, where it did drive them was to high school. Although public high schools had existed for more than 110 years, 1933 was the first year a majority of people whom we now deem to be of high school age were actually enrolled. It was a terrible time for this development, as most U.S. public schools are supported by local property tax revenues, which plummeted along with land values during the Depression. As a result, schools had little choice but to see themselves as custodial institutions for a high percentage of their students, an attitude that has never entirely disappeared. Nevertheless, public high school became, by default, a nearly universal experience for American youth.

Young people who attended high school had always appeared more juvenile than their counterparts who went to work. Suddenly, all young people in their teens seemed younger than they ever had before. Parents, who until this time depended on their children to help support the household, now became accustomed to viewing them as dependents until the age of eighteen. When the economy started to improve in the late

103

a recognition, if not serious consideration, of distinct social classes in the benignly incompetent world of Riverdale High School. Superman, despite its Nietzschean overtones, derived its emotional power by appealing to young men's secret fantasies of possessing great powers that had scarcely been tapped. Frank Sinatra, the first true teen idol, was admittedly a far more sexual figure than Rooney. But in his early years, he seemed so thin and vulnerable, crooning in his bow tie, that his female fans wanted to mother him (think Leonardo DiCaprio.) Like Rooney, Sinatra also later married Ava Gardner. Unlike Rooney, he eventually grew into a compellingly mature man— in his style, if not always in his behavior. But first he proved that an "unfinished" man could be very attractive indeed.

Mickey Rooney with Lyn and Lee Wilde in *Andy Hardy's Blonde Trouble*, 1944, directed by George B. Seitz

1930s, parents were able to provide their children with a little more spending money for their social lives. The first Andy Hardy movie, a low-budget, so-called B movie released in 1937, struck pay dirt. It drew large audiences, and it helped mark the emergence of high school–centered youth culture (as opposed to the pre-Depression youth culture of the jazz age, which was focused on college). It was becoming obvious that even though teenagers were no longer viewed as a necessary and responsible part of the workforce, they were eager, willing, energetic consumers. These young people were oddly threatening because, like Mickey Rooney's character, they were growing into a new and almost alien entity. But, more significantly, they were also profitable.

Several avatars of teen culture who emerged during the early 1940s have been surprisingly enduring. Archie essentially transplanted Andy Hardy's world into comic book form. This new dimension was

By bringing an end to the Depression, World War II helped bring youth culture into being. But it also interrupted the aforementioned trend. Fighting in the war was a maturing experience, and the generation who went into battle developed a style that, while derided as conformist, was nevertheless extremely masculine and fully mature.

The current American fascination with these men, as documented in Tom Brokaw's best-selling book *The Greatest Generation*, stems in large part from a belief that these were the last fully evolved grown-ups America produced. They seem to those of us who were born later to be more comfortable in their identities than we can ever hope to be.

During the decades following World War II, the psychologist Erik Erikson focused Americans on the challenge of forging an identity, coining the term *identity crisis* — now virtually an all-purpose catchphrase. Erikson argued that the purpose of one's adolescent years is to discover who you are, to understand the society of which you are a part, and to define your role within it, which you will play for the rest of your life. Erikson acknowledged the forces of change, but he nevertheless assumed it possible to forge a useful identity that can last a lifetime. And, in 1950s America, with its stable political environment, its huge, rather paternalistic corporations, it probably was possible.

But since Erikson's time, the end of adolescence has grown ever more elusive. Employers demand more and more education for jobs that are little more challenging, and far less stable, than those available a generation ago. Inflation-adjusted wages of today's college graduates approximate those of high school graduates in 1970. The years of a man's economic maturity, which began to shrink during the 1930s, have continued to shrink, and those years are increasingly

precarious. Society denies us a stable identity, and we are encouraged to define ourselves not by who we are or what we do but by what we buy.

, And because the goal of a consumer economy is, after all, to goad its members into consumption, it follows that our prosperity depends largely on the denial of identity. If we spend in order to figure out who we are, it is important that we not find the answer—which would mean that we would stop spending. It is important that we look into the mirror and see that we have not become great, or even complete. Our identities are adrift—somewhere between the juvenile and the senile: modern life has made Mickeys of us all.

Mickey Rooney with Les Girls in a scene from the film *Sound Off*, 1951, directed by Richard Quine

MEN OF MARBLE

Photographs by Roberto Schezen

Epic Forms,
Stadio dei Marmi,
Rome, 1996-97.
Photos by
Roberto Schezen

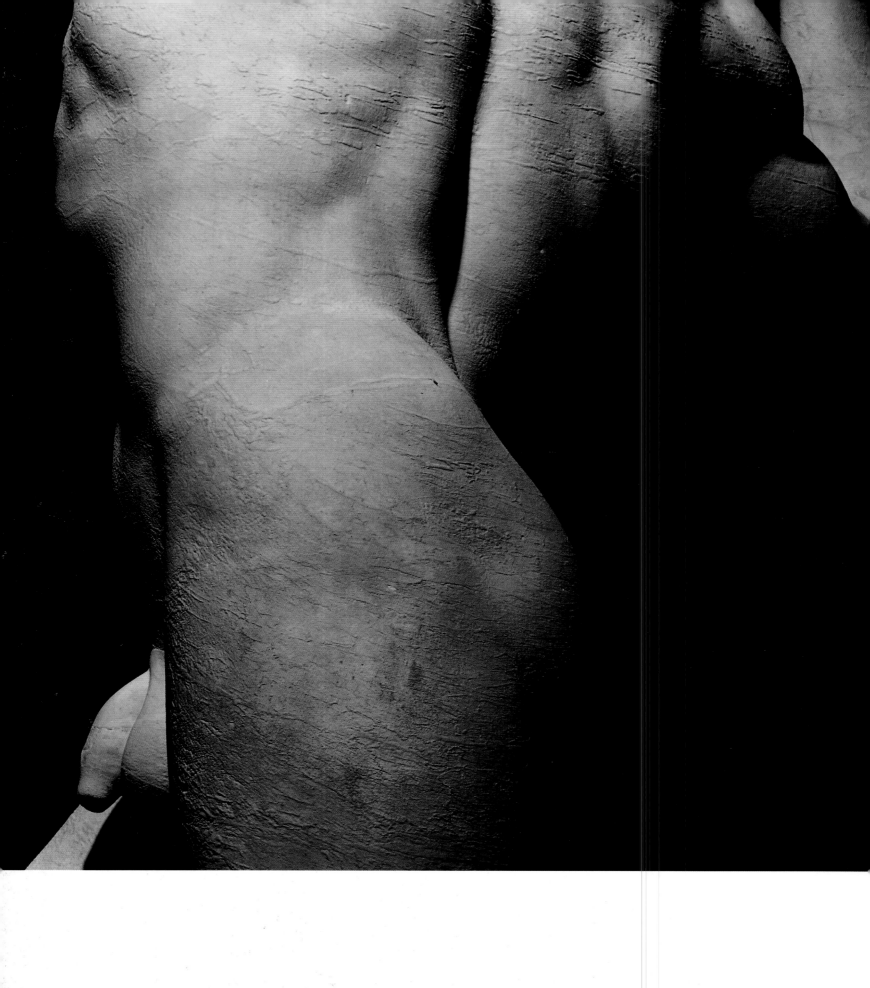

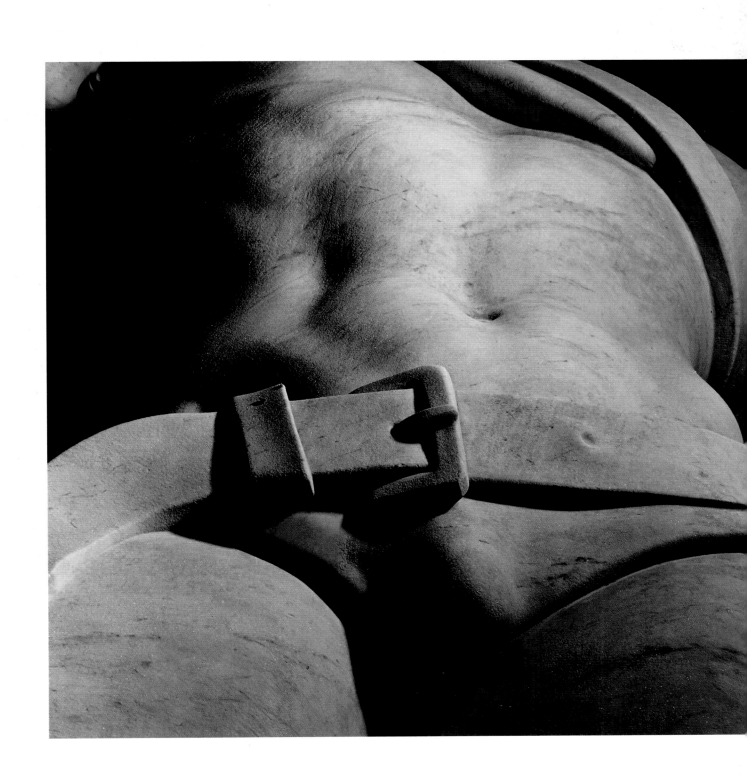

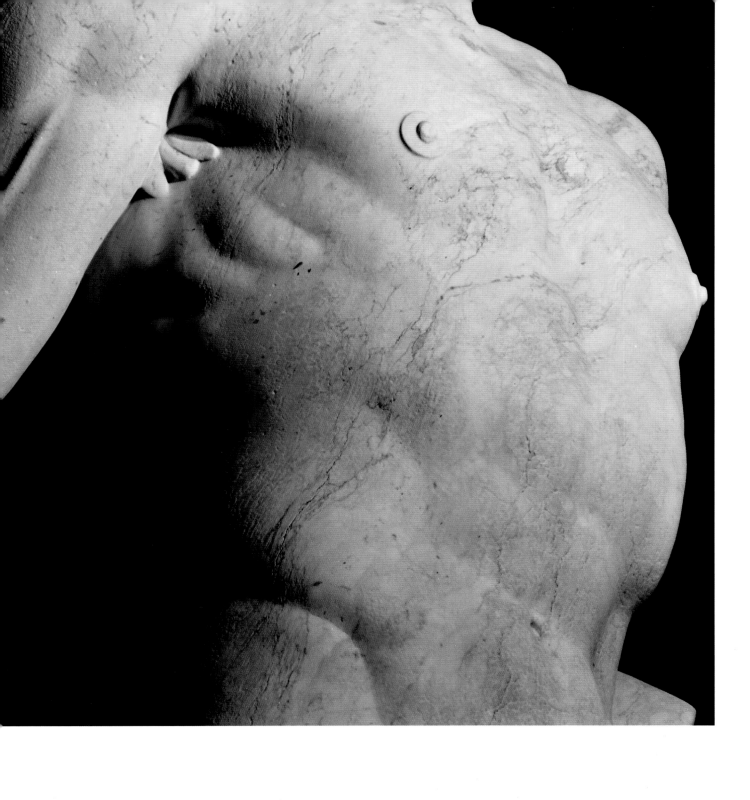

Ugo Volli

ODYSSEUS AND MALE CUNNING

Myths and Images of Masculinity in Western Culture

Being a man is hard work. This has always been true in the Western tradition. The work in question involves education, training, and, especially, selection. Because, according to this tradition, not all human beings are men, not even all those of the male gender. Humanity, that is, the masculine quality of being a man, was characterized by opposition right from the start.

For the ancient Greeks, the first to develop a theory of the required education of man (the *paideia* that Jaeger studied), being a man meant first of all being male, but also being free and not a slave, an adult and not a child, a member of the community and not an outsider, and endowed with the physical, cultural, and mental wherewithal to fulfill one's responsibilities toward family, local community, state, and religion, and hence not poverty-stricken.

The consequence of this privileged state and of the education received is that a man is firm and knows how to face human and natural adversities with calm self-control, preserving his status and his dignity, being able to impose himself with intelligence and strength.

A man, in the Western tradition that begins with the Greeks, was autonomous, in the etymological sense of setting one's own laws, being, that is, at once free and responsible, not caught up in the variable forces of impulses and desires, but rather constant and in control of oneself. Michel Foucault has written an extremely interesting book about the counterpoint, extremely common in Greek philosophy, between *hedonai*, or pleasures, and *encrateia*, self-control. A man controls himself and is capable of foreseeing the results of his own actions. A man is generally thought of as a citizen, a political animal; primarily as a function of his self-control and his control of his family and of a given economic setting. Ideally, he is a small landholder. It is significant that the first book of Aristotle's *Politics* should be devoted to *chrematistike*, a theory of home economics that a landlord must understand in order to preserve intact his estate and his liberty. From Roman law, which gave full liberty to the *paterfamilias*, right up to the census-driven electoral legislation that was standard in most European countries until the first few decades of the twentieth century, the identification of a man as a well-to-do citizen was practically universal and always motivated by considerations of self-control.

Well before Greek philosophers, we find an inaugural figure, in the Greek tradition, who incarnates this capacity for self-control, along with the drive for expansion, the will to dominate that is characteristic of Western man. This figure is Odysseus.

Pellegrino Tibaldi, *Ulysses and the Sorceress Circe*, central section with Ulysses and his comrades, 1554. Bologna, Palazzo Poggi

115

This character is marked by his powerful identity and his isolation from his fellow adventurers, a difference that is emphasized by the epithets that are repeatedly used to describe him: *polytropos*, *polymetis*, *polyphronos*, *polymechanos*. All are adjectives that allude to a certain intensification, but perhaps also literally to a multiplication, a diversification, of the mental faculties. What sets Odysseus apart from the other Homeric heroes is not actually a superior intelligence or understanding, as much as his "cunning" (*metis*), the ability to invent tricks and stratagems in order to attain his ends, a control over himself and his environment.

"*Metis*, as a common noun, refers to a particular type of intelligence, an informed prudence," write Marcel Detienne and Jean-Pierre Vernant in the opening of their book, *Cunning Intelligence in Greek Culture and Society* (1978). "*Metis* is a type of intelligence and of thought, a way of knowing; it implies a complex but very coherent body of mental attitudes and intellectual behavior which combine flair, wisdom, forethought, subtlety of mind, resourcefulness, vigilance, opportunism, various skills, and experience acquired over the years. It is applied to

structure of Western man, let us compare two well-known and psychologically parallel episodes from Homeric poetry: Achilles' willingness to refrain from the use of arms to oppose Agamemnon in book I of the Iliad, and Odysseus' willingness to refrain from immediately punishing his "maids" as they "whore" with the suitors in book XX of the Odyssey.

The episode that commences the narrative of the Iliad is Apollo's request (supported by the very solid considerations of an epidemic in the Greek camp) that the young girl Chryseis, awarded to Agamemnon as a prize of war, should be returned to her father, a priest of Apollo. After some resistance, the chief of the Greek expedition agrees, but demands in exchange Briseis, another lovely slave of war who had been awarded to Achilles. There ensues a violent argument with a free exchange of threats. When Agamemnon finally announces that he is going to seize the girl by main force, in spite of the "strike" announced by Achilles,

. . . anguish gripped Achilles.
The heart in his rugged chest was pounding, torn ...
Should he draw the long sharp sword slung at his hip,
Thrust through the ranks and kill Agamemnon now?—
or check his rage and beat his fury down?
(Iliad I, 188-193)

Odysseus in book XX of the Odyssey finds himself in a similar state of rage, as he "lay . . . awake, alert" in the entrance hall of his own house, on the eve of the slaughter of the suitors, "plotting within himself the suitors' death," while

As the women slipped from the house,
the maids who whored in the suitors' beds each night,
tittering, linking arms and frisking as before.
The master's anger rose inside his chest,
torn in thought, debating, head and heart—
should he up and rush them, kill them one and all
or let them rut with their lovers one last time?
The heart inside him growled low with rage,
as a bitch mounting over her weak defenseless puppies
growls, facing a stranger, bristling for a showdown—
so he growled from his depths, hackles rising at their
     outrage. (Odyssey XX, 6-17)

One may note a slight difference in the states of uncertainty of the two heroes. In the first case, it is the heart, physically considered "inside the chest" (the word actually used in the Greek here is not *kardía* but *etor*, a rare term) that is uncertain (the verb is *mermerizein*); in the second case, it is Odysseus who is uncertain (again, *mermerizein*) in his heart and in his soul, that is, head and heart (*katà phrena kai katà thumon*). These are traditional formulas, repeated a thousand times in Homer, which we might well consider equivalent or irrelevant were it not

situations which are transient, shifting, disconcerting, and ambiguous, situations which do not lend themselves to precise measurement, exact calculation, or rigorous logic. Now, in the picture of thought and intelligence presented by the philosophers, the professional experts where intelligence was concerned, all the qualities of mind which go to make up *metis*, its sleights of hand, its resourceful ploys and its stratagems, are usually thrust into the shadows, erased from the realm of true knowledge and relegated, according to the circumstances, to the level of mere routine, chancy inspiration, changeable opinion or even *charlatanerie*, pure and simple."

In order to better understand just what this *metis* is and what relationship it establishes with the mental

Pellegrino Tibaldi, *Ulysses Blinds Polyphemus*, 1554. Bologna, Palazzo Poggi

The white-armed goddess Hera sped me down:
she loves you both, she cares for you both alike.
Stop this fighting, now. Don't lay hand to sword.
Lash him with threats of the price that he will face.
And I tell you this—and I know it is the truth—
one day glittering gifts will lie before you,
three times over to pay for all his outrage.
Hold back now. Obey us both."
                            So she urged
and the swift runner complied at once: "I must—
when the two of you hand down commands, Goddess,
a man submits though his heart breaks with fury.
Better for him by far. If a man obeys the gods
they're quick to hear his prayers."
                            And with that
Achilles stayed his burly hand on the silver hilt
and slid the huge blade back in its sheath.
He would not fight the orders of Athena.
(Iliad I, 193-222)

We have here a typical reconstruction of a decision-making process that is entirely external, in which there is no subject, but the pressure of the "grief" that "comes" (*geneto*). The passions that unsettle organs of sensibility, viewed as physical and passive, are opposed by the still entirely external intervention of the goddess. Quite different is the narrative of Odysseus's reaction to his doubts concerning what action to take:

But he struck his chest and curbed his fighting heart:
"Bear up, old heart! You've borne worse, far worse,
that day when the Cyclops, man-mountain, bolted
your hardy comrades down. But you held fast—
Nobody but your cunning pulled you through
the monster's cave you thought would be your death."

Pellegrino
Tibaldi,
*Ulysses and
Cyclops*, detail
showing the
flight of the
comrades, 1554.
Bologna, Palazzo
Poggi

facing page:
Pellegrino
Tibaldi,
*Ulysses's
Comrades
Stealing
the Oxen of the
Sun*, detail,
1554. Bologna,
Palazzo Poggi

that the internal nature of Odysseus's uncertainty had been emphasized in the introduction of the comparison: the heart (this time it is called *kradíe*) growled low inside him (that is, *endon*).

This is not the central point, however. In the face of uncertainty, the decision made by Achilles takes place in a wholly traditional manner, that is, through divine intervention:

As his racing spirit veered back and forth,
just as he drew his huge blade from its sheath,
down from the vaulting heavens swept Athena,
the white-armed goddess Hera sped her down:
Hera loved both men and cared for both alike.
Rearing behind him Pallas seized his fiery hair—
only Achilles saw her, none of the other fighters—
struck with wonder he spun around, he knew her at once,
Pallas Athena! the terrible blazing of those eyes,
and his winged words went flying: "Why, why now?
Child of Zeus with the shield of thunder, why come now?
To witness the outrage Agamemnon just committed?
I tell you this, and so help me it's the truth—
he'll soon pay for his arrogance with his life!"
    Her gray eyes clear, the goddess Athena answered,
"Down from the skies I come to check your rage
if only you will yield.

So he forced his spirit in submission,
the rage in his breast reined back—unswerving,
all endurance. But he himself kept tossing, turning. . . .
(Odyssey XX, 17-30)

Odysseus here performs functions that in the case of
the episode of Briseis (and, in general, throughout the
course of the Homeric epics) are attributed to the gods;
he himself thinks, decides, curbs himself. It is no accident
that often we find reference made to him with the epithet
"divine" (*theoios*) and, even more often, with that of
"luminous" (*dios*), related to the root of the name of Zeus.
Odysseus's capacity to make his own decisions is
underscored by the fact that in this episode as well we
find the apparition of a deity, Athena herself, who had
stopped Achilles by pulling on his hair, and who often
protects Odysseus in various ways. But this time she
appears after the decision has already been made, and
she does no more than to encourage and calm the hero,
giving him the gift of a good night's sleep.

Our task here, naturally, is neither to engage in
literary criticism of the Homeric corpus nor to analyze the
"actual" history of Greek civilization; nor are we even
interested in characterizing the transition between the two
episodes that we are discussing as "progress." But there
can be no question that there was a clear transition, a
decisive shift in the way in which the action is portrayed
and described in terms of its relationship to the
protagonist, a narrative shift that entailed a change in the
conception of human beings and a shift in the experience
that living and breathing human beings had of themselves.
To feel that one is guided by the gods is certainly quite
different from attributing to oneself a personal capacity to
choose and decide. It is certainly in this new perception of
self-control that we find the origin of the temperance
(*sophrosyne*) that is the most typical and common virtue in
the Greek tradition: a virtue that did not imply goodness of
intent, generosity, love of one's neighbor, or willingness to
forgive—but rather a clear-eyed capacity to calculate one's
own best interests and to seize the opportune moment
(*kairos*) for action. Odysseus does not forgive the maids;
indeed, he has them all hanged at the end of the poem.
His virtue does not consist in some form of goodness, but
rather in the control he exerts over his own passions,
making him into something like a machine of war. This
marks the beginning of a story that was to have vast
repercussions in European culture and determine a
fundamental cultural model, the Western model of virility,
consisting not only of strength, but also of self-awareness,
cunning, concealed aggressiveness, and knowledge.

Let us examine things more closely. It is Odysseus
who speaks, or at least some form of "subject" that exists
within him; he is, however, sufficiently extraneous to his
own heart (*kradie*) that he can reprove it and curb it: it is
his heart that must "bear up" and "submit" and "expect
death"; his comrades, on the other hand, are "his own,"
while his cunning is yet another matter, mentioned in the
third person. The "heart," which bears anguish, is subject
to rage, and fears death is the seat of feelings and
passions, evidently; but it has a powerful bond to his body,
it is "curbed" by Odysseus "striking his chest," and, after
the decision is made, it is responsible for causing the hero
to "keep tossing, turning" in his cot. *Metis* is a technical
skill, a form of know-how, a calculating thought, to use the
terminology of contemporary philosophy, which "frees" one
from the traps of adventure and is the necessary premise
for *sophrosyne*. Odysseus himself is often described as
"*polymetis*," rich in cunning or endowed with a mind that
knows many wiles and tricks. We must therefore suppose
that *metis* is here considered to be an inner and specific
faculty or manner of Odysseus's intellect, something that he
has also "ingested," not unlike Zeus, in the myth recounted
by Hesiod, who swallowed the goddess Metis, his wife, and
took advice from her whilst she was within him.

If we think back to the episode of Polyphemus, to the
episode that we are discussing, and to other very famous
episodes, such as that of the construction of the Trojan
Horse or that of the song of the Sirens, we can easily
agree that, in the first place, *metis* is the ability to offer
the world an appropriate surface of significance, that is,
to take on an external aspect that does not correspond
to one's own inner reality (whether that reality be
emotional or historical) but that is opportune given the

specific situation, ideally suited to a certain plan of action. Odysseus escapes from the cavern of Polyphemus by hiding himself under the belly of the sheep that the blinded giant allows to leave the cave; the Trojan Horse works in much the same manner, concealing in its interior a band of warriors who will expunge the city; in the case of Penelope's handmaidens the mask is more abstract, but equally effective: Odysseus does not give in to the rage that would betray him, but instead pretends to be calm and asleep, preserving, in short, the disguise as a beggar that he uses as a shield to pass unobserved among his enemies. *Metis*, in order to be calculating reason, must also be dissimulation, a semiotic machine for the construction of appearances. It is not so much a matter of lying, here, because one's word is not at play, but rather a question of mounting an array of effects of meaning, causing others at once to believe and not to know, to establish an appearance that conceals a secret. This type of operation demands an array of imitations, an effect of mimesis.

This link between appearance and secret is crucial to the displacement that we are trying to trace. A hero decides to offer the world a deceptive signifying surface, but beneath that surface is concealed and remains the plan that engendered it. There is thus created a two-level structure, made up of an appearance and a plan, a phantom and a design. Unquestionably, this is a semiotic structure that has something in common with the traditional breakdown of the sign into signifier and significance—except that here the significance is qualified inasmuch as it is in conflict with the signifier; or, perhaps we should say, the signifier is created especially to conceal its "significance."

These considerations lead us immediately to another important characteristic of the new form of analysis found in the actions of Odysseus. This characteristic requires some degree of planning, a capacity to foresee the future within certain limitations and to envision clearly the consequences of one's own actions. As he recounted the episode of Polyphemus to Alcinous (Odyssey IX), Odysseus explained more clearly the "forbearance" that curbs his heart in the passage that we are examining here. When Polyphemus devoured the first comrades of Odysseus and then fell asleep, full and content, the hero was tempted to kill the giant immediately, but he realized (once again, on his own, without divine assistance) that he would thus be unable to get out of the cavern; he therefore decided to wait:

And I with my fighting heart, I thought at first
to steal up to him, draw the sharp sword at my hip
and stab his chest where the midriff packs the liver—
I groped for the fatal spot but a fresh thought held me back.

There at a stroke we'd finish off ourselves as well—
how could we with our bare hands heave back
that slab he set to block his cavern's gaping maw?
So we lay there groaning, waiting Dawn's first light.
(Odyssey IX, 299-306)

Along with the future of planning, in fact, the past of experience is also available to a man endowed with *metis*. We see this very clearly in the passage that we are now analyzing. In order to persuade his heart to bear up under its wrath, Odysseus remembers a moment from the past and compares the two situations—that of the past and the present one—in an explicit manner. The presence, in the womb of the present time, of both future and past as dimensions of planning and identity, is one of the dominant themes in the existential analysis of Heidegger and, in general, in the conception of time that derives from Husserlian analysis. Consider, for instance, the following, from paragraph 79 of *Being and Time*: "Inasmuch as it calculates, plans, foresees, and anticipates, the *Dasein* [Being] always says already, whether explicitly or not: "then" this will happen, "before" that has been completed, "now" we must redo that which "then" was not successfully completed."

One last element should be emphasized: the nature of decision itself, the capacity to unify all of the behavior of a single person, in short, to "command," to "use the body as a tool," as Plato was to put it a few centuries later. Odysseus's heart obeys its subject (itself) just as Achilles obeys the goddess, without even being able to object; it possesses, then, a more absolute power than even the deity, who is required to ask for obedience in a polite manner (*ai ke pithetai*, Iliad I, 207) and make promises in exchange.

Nowadays, we have a hard time comprehending the difficulties associated with the figure of man, head of a family, legislator, and perhaps hero. This difficulty has many causes: natural adversities have been greatly tamed by technology; the state has eliminated most of the risks involved in human interactions; egalitarianism has eliminated most of the barriers of gender, class, religion, and race that once made attaining the full status of manhood so problematic and exclusive. But for millennia, the condition of manhood implied a network of obligations, rights, and attitudes, which constituted the main object of education, including religious and philosophical education, and at the same time the foundation of all political order. The virile ideal that emerges from the accounts of the Spanish conquistadores of South America, as well as the masculine image found in the novels of Conrad (for example, in "Shadow-Line: A Confession") or Western movies, continued along the same line—in sharp contrast, of course, with that of feminine identity, which formed in Western culture in a different manner and with clearly opposing contents.

In order to understand the importance of this process, we should begin with one of the most celebrated studies in

120

Pellegrino Tibaldi, *Neptune and the Ship of Ulysses*, 1554. Bologna, Palazzo Poggi

anthropology, Margaret Mead's *Sex and Temperament in Three Primitive Societies*. Mead concludes from her studies in New Guinea that the relationship between personality structure and biological gender is variable, and depends upon the ways in which a society is organized, even though the opposite sexes are found universally in humanity.

Western society, on the basis of its Greek origins and its Hebraic foundations (which could not be discussed in this limited space), opted for one of these possible definitions: that men should attempt to resemble Odysseus, emulating his self-control and his intelligence. This way of being male requires an education, a training of the character, certain techniques of the self. This is an idea that emerges in Western thought as early as Plato, in the *Charmides*, for instance, and especially in the *Alcibiades* II.

Self-instruction, the cultivation of virtue, according to Plato, is a political matter. In the face of the overweening power of the Persians and Spartans, the military superpowers of the period, only chiefs capable of perfect self-control could offer Athens a chance at survival. If a man requires power (at least a certain amount of power) in order to be considered a man, the reverse is also true: power, in order to prevail, requires the virility of a man, requires the splendid but also dark virtues of Odysseus. This definition of virility as self-awareness and as *metis* (cunning intelligence) has been one of the underlying political reasons for the strength and aggressiveness of the West. That it should now be called into question by the voices of other cultures and other visions of humanity constitutes a great and perhaps irreversible historical revolution. It is a rich and fertile paradox that this should have happened in the wake of its (excessive) victories, not in the aftermath of a defeat.

Note: All Homeric translation by Robert Fagles

Carlo Bertelli

MASCULINE ART

Universality and the Boundaries of Gender in Art

The feminist polemic and, in its wake, the creation of gender history, have designated art history as primarily masculine, overweening, and autocratic, with a tendency toward abuse of power. The eighteenth-century presumption of art as a universal phenomenon was attacked as new identities for art proliferated: art as feminine, art as homosexual, and, inevitably, art as masculine or male-sexist. At the last Venice Biennale, a Milanese artist, Monica Bonvicini, isolated herself from the rest of the event by constructing her own closed space, on the walls of which she denounced the sex-crazed prejudices of male thought, with reference to Le Corbusier, whom she accused of thinking of architecture in masculine terms.

Feminists and gay artists have almost invariably failed to generate new esthetic canons with claims to universality, nor could they, since their rebellion originated within the art system, which is no longer merely a set of guidelines to the making of art, but a complex network that now accommodates manifestations that would once have been alien, "outsider" phenomena.

Particularly representative of a spuriously universalist masculine conception of art is the male artist's treatment of the relationship between painter or sculptor and female model, often presented as a metaphor for art itself. In some cases, the female model contemplates the work of the master. Thus, in *The*

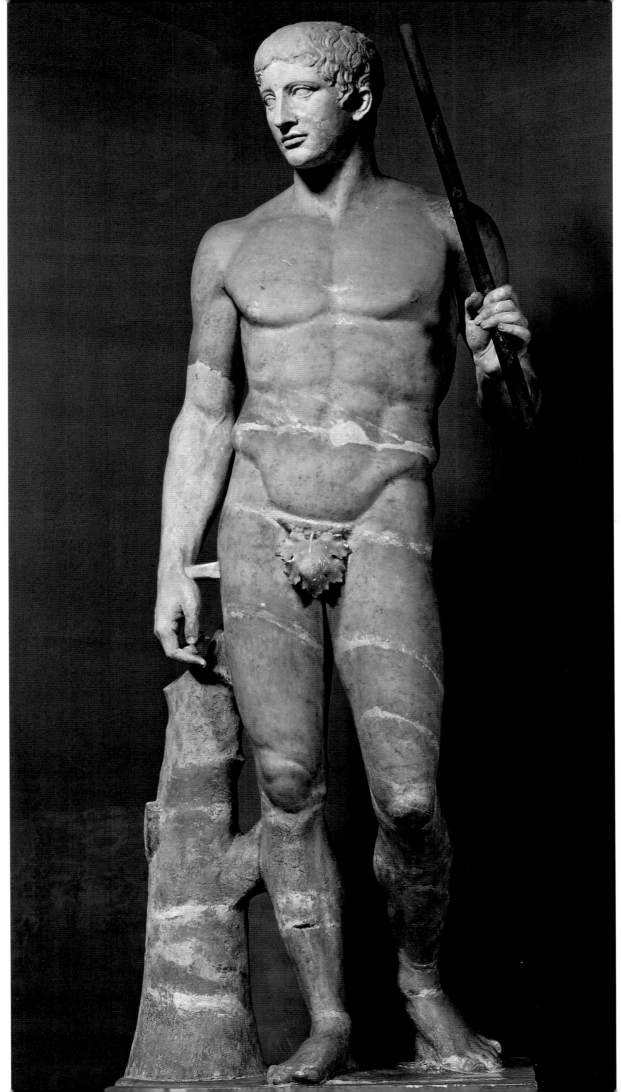

Polycletus,
Doriphore.
Vatican,
New Wing

facing page:
Pompeo Batoni,
Sacred Heart.
Rome, Church
of the Gesù

123

124

Michael Keaton
in *Batman*,
1989, directed
by Tim Burton.
Set photograph

facing page:
Jean-Auguste-
Dominique
Ingres, *Raphael
and La
Fornarina*.
Columbus,
Gallery
of Fine Arts

Painter's Studio: A Real Allegory Summing Up Seven Years of My Life (1854-55) by Gustave Courbet, the model ("*une modèle de femme nue*," as the artist himself explained) stands behind the painter and watches as he paints a landscape. Amidst the crowd of friends and enemies that Courbet distributed on both sides in the painting, the nude woman, a boy, and a cat are the only ones closely observing the artist. Eve looks, nostalgic and languid, at the paradise lost that the painter re-creates for a moment, the instant of our life, before her eyes.

A variation on this theme is found in Jean-Auguste-Dominique Ingres's painting *Raphael and La Fornarina* (c. 1814), portraying the Italian artist and his mistress, a baker's daughter. Ingres here identified himself with Raphael, since the painter in the painting and the painter who makes the painting are both thinking about the connection between artistic creation and erotic relationships. Whereas Courbet's painting within the

construction of art in accordance with male canons.)

One hundred years later, Pablo Picasso depicted this established symbolic relationship, giving it a slightly different portrayal, according to his own artistic style. He, too, depicts a woman and an image of this same woman, both within the same artwork. But in Picasso's version, the woman is shown caught in rapt contemplation of her own image, which is translated into the antirealistic visual language of the artist. The artist himself is completely removed, and the artwork serves as his stand-in. The act of making art, the process of abstraction, defamiliarization, and intellectualization, is the work of the male artist; the woman is both the passive object of inspiration and, subsequently, the passive appreciator.

In Picasso's etchings, the artist often appears in the role of mentor, at times sharing with the model the joy of creation. The erotic relationship in these works is stronger than simply an undertone. One might say that artist and model together created the work, which is

painting is a landscape, in Ingres's painting the interior work is actually a portrait of La Fornarina herself. The lover-qua-model sits in the great artist's lap. He, however, does not look at her but instead gazes with pride at his portrait of her: he appears to be more enamored of his own re-creation than of the woman herself. La Fornarina, for her part, aware that she is being admired and tenderly protective of her young friend, looks toward us, foretelling a future in which Raphael—or, at least, Ingres's painting of Raphael—will belong to us more than to her. (Ingres here confirms that while desire is an essential component of male sexuality, the sublimation of desire is essential to the

Dancing Faun.
Pompeii, Casa
del Fauno

126

thus their daughter. Or the work of art, in visual terms
unlike the true woman, actually reveals to the woman
her true and intimate essence. But again, the operation
is masculine, leaving the woman to regard herself in
a particularly perceptive mirror.

In a 1906 painting by Francis Picabia, the model
stands in front of an entire wall covered with canvases in
the studio of artist Fernand Cormon. Perhaps someone
is painting her portrait. Picabia creates a parallel
between this fantastic array of paintings and the model:
she, too, is a work of art, or an object to be turned into
one. The lone woman is not a creator, and the world of
art is inaccessible to her.

Picasso focused on and emphasized this theme to
the point of obsession and exasperation. The masculinity
of the artist was exalted in the metamorphosis of
the painter into a Silenus or a Minotaur, and in later
compositions the relationship became explicitly and
exaggeratedly carnal. Repeatedly, and especially in his
later years, Picasso fragmented the unity of the female
body, establishing an almost autonomous placement of
the female genitalia, transforming it into a shining sun.

This masculine aggression is found throughout art.
In radically different forms, but in a conception that
is not too far distant, Hans Bellmer's menacing dolls rid
the female anatomy of all body parts except those that
are sexual and obviously erotic. British painting, in its
most realistic phases with Lucian Freud, offered pitiless
geographic and documentary depictions of the nude
female body. The women in these paintings look as
if they had been violently stripped, forced into torturous
poses, and then painted as if they were bellwethers
of death. Painters of the German Renaissance had
sarcastically insisted on the vanity of female beauty,
cruelly juxtaposing the physical deterioration of old age
with the flourishing beauty of youth. Let us recall that
in Eden, Adam was given the tree of life, but Eve was
given the tree of knowledge. Eve offered Adam the fruit
of knowledge, a fruit that was to undo them both.

Radically changing styles have not vitiated masculine
aggressiveness in art. Claes Oldenburg's enormous

Monica Bonvicini, *I Believe in the Skin of Things as in That of Women (Credo nella pelle delle cose come in quella delle donne)*, 1999. Venice Biennale, 48th International Exposition of Art

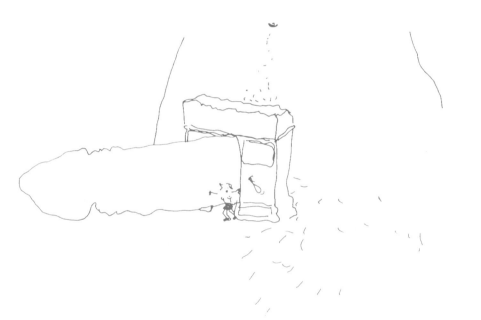

sculptures of a pocketknife and lipstick are both obviously phallic images, although the pocketknife is a stereotypically male "accessory" and lipstick is female. His humorous images, so opposite in what they traditionally signify, become allied, paralleled, similar in visual representation.

If a cadre of artists continues to stake claims for a universal language of art in our century, the retreat of the masculine—in life as in art—has also been evident, for example, in the decline of the hero.

During the formation of modern Europe, Thomas Carlyle published a series of lectures in 1841, titled *On Heroes, Hero-Worship, and The Heroic in History*, that offered a great myth upon which to construct the various national celebrations of unity, justifying and demanding sacrifices from private citizens on behalf of collective virtue. Like demigods, heroes—in the mythology of Carlyle—stood up against the horizon, presenting examples that would energize the multitudes, dictating new forms of behavior. These are the prophets, rulers, priests, and poets who blaze new paths with their noble and solitary deeds.

The masculine identity of the hero has since faded. The history of war—and art—is replete with military heroes, whose exploits are celebrated and honored. The war hero of the end of the twentieth century can hardly be counted with his noble predecessors. Two Italian pilots captured during the Gulf War became heroes, as did three American soldiers made prisoners during the war waged by NATO against the Yugoslav Federal Republic. Even though there was no heroic action to portray, those who represented them and elevated them to the Valhalla of heroes were their mothers, sisters, and aunts, who filled television screens, first fearful and later exultant. The pacifism of Lysistrata is replaced by televisual pride, which reabsorbs the hero into the comfortable context of a family pacified by the opportunity offered to emerge from anonymity. Space heroes, too, are distinguished by the degree to which we are more familiar with their families—shown gathered on sofas in their living room, anxious to be interviewed—rather than the astronauts themselves, who are usually somewhere off circling the globe, their voices crackling

Gustave Courbet,
*The Artist's
Studio*. Paris,
Musée d'Orsay

facing page:
Gilbert & George,
Naked Suits,
1994

David Hamilton,
*Just what is it
that makes
today's homes
so different, so
appealing?*, 1956

over the phone from their distant capsules, anxious for news from earth and from their famous families.

Half a century of peace in Europe, American popular opposition to the war in Vietnam, and wars in which highly technological weapons minimize the losses to Western armies have destroyed this Romantic figure. It may very well be that under Allied bombardment of Kosovo, there were acts of heroism on the part of soldiers or civilians. All of that, however, is out of our line of sight, just as the fighters of Chiapas, Kashmir, or Iraq are invisible to us. In terms of image, they are no different—though their fates are not even comparable—from the invisible heroes represented by the female members of their anxious families.

The disappearance of masculinity can be seen in other contemporary myths. Twentieth-century superheroes such as Batman and Superman may even have a small version of themselves at their side, a very young Robin or Superboy, but their relationship with the women that sometimes aid them in their adventures, or even save their lives, remains unresolved from one episode to the next. In order to be accepted by the woman that—perhaps—he loves, Superman must take care not to reveal his own superior nature; instead he must present himself as weak and mild-mannered. He is certainly not Zeus, who descends upon Danae as a rain of gold, or who as a satyr takes advantage of the sleeping nymph. Sexuality is rigorously suppressed in the escapades of these heroes (or superheroes).

If the absolute dominance of masculine conceptions in the idealistic treatment of art as a universal manifestation of the spirit is beginning to be uprooted, it is not merely thanks to a theoretical (feminist or gay) discourse but, at a deeper level, by the collapse of the traditional relations between the sexes. The scientific possibility of human cloning cannot fail to form part of our outlook, while the now-routine practice of organ transplants presents us with an unlimited extension of the human body, which accepts or rejects complementary components from other bodies according to criteria that are, in most cases, no longer sexual. Thus, while our bodies become universal, our minds still try to maintain their separate sexual identities by erecting new barricades.

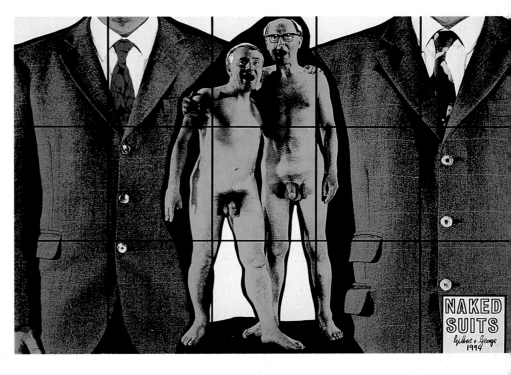

While for many centuries art focused on sexual relations between men and women, introducing such themes as virginity, faithfulness, promiscuity, visibility of the body, liberty, or segregation of the sexes, the art of the future will probably have little or nothing to do with the couple or the family or the imposition of masculine norms of behavior on the other half of humanity. Issues such as artificial fertilization and even cloning are harbingers of what is to come. The possibility of asexual reproduction of humans is scientifically realistic and, precisely because it is becoming a genuine possibility, will become the subject of a painful moral consideration.

If these are to be central themes, art can scarcely fail to deal with them. The dematerialization of sexual relations and the uncertainties concerning the boundaries of life correspond to two phenomena, one intrinsic to art, the other permeating society.

The intrinsic phenomenon, on the one hand, is the progressive erosion, over the course of the century, of manual skill in the arts, corresponding to an exaltation of almost crude expression ("informal" art, "Art Brut") and a turning to the body as a means to a recovery of a total physicality. The social phenomenon, on the other, is the virtual cult of political correctness, a prudent and self-censoring attitude capable of sucking energy and authenticity from the statements and expressions of artists. The manifestation of masculinity, which runs the risk of provoking accusations of sexism, has become far less explicit as a result. In any case, the self-declaration of masculinity leads to a questioning of the ("masculine") universality of art.

Claudio Risé

THERE IS A SAVAGE IN THE FUTURE OF MAN

The Necessity of Masculine Archetypes

Men in Difficulty

At the end of this century and this millennium, men, as portrayed by the mass media, seem to be in a pretty sorry state. First of all, some people say, their brains seem to be inferior. In fact, communication between the right and left hemispheres is faster and more complete in the female brain, according to Paolo Pancheri, professor of psychiatry at the University La Sapienza in Rome.

Men, moreover, are sexually unnecessary. Women are now scientifically able to reproduce on their own: all they have to do is exercise this power and males—according to respected scientists working on female genetic engineering—"are likely to wind up on reservations." Not to mention the fact that, according to Professor Luc Montagnier, one of the discoverers of the AIDS virus, in the world of tomorrow, once we have conquered the retrovirus, we will conquer death itself, and it will no longer be necessary to reproduce at all, much less sexually. Last, males are economically unproductive and not very enterprising. For instance, in the U.S. most of the new companies are founded by women; in Europe for now that is true in only 30 percent of the cases, but the trend is growing sharply. So the men of today look pretty hapless.

We should also keep in mind a series of social and clinical phenomena. For instance: reluctance to leave home and to marry and proliferating phobias of every

sort. Growing numbers of men do not take out driver's licenses, won't go to public offices, are unable to keep track of their own finances, and delegate everything to wife, girlfriend, or mother. Last, the growing rate of sterility, a somatic expression of the fear of fathering children: as of this writing, some 40 percent of Western white males are incapable of fertilizing an ovum.

In the face of this gender disaster, many observers feel that the male is an endangered species or at least an endangered gender, a weak animal overcome by the harsh struggle of natural selection. The most optimistic admit that men might survive, but in a subordinate role to women, like Third-World immigrants in Europe during the colonial era, second-class citizens in an advanced society.

Men in Movement

And yet there are signs of change. In the United States, the "men's movement" is by now a vast universe, capable of mobilizing more people than the traditional political parties and the trade unions. This constellation ranges from the Christian movement of the Promise Keepers to the Black Muslims led by Louis Farrakhan, and on to the more peaceful followers of the intellectual guru of the American men's movement, the poet Robert Bly, whose book *Iron John* was a longtime best-seller. In Europe, too,

books that describe in positive terms the "male question" are selling out edition after edition, and spontaneous movements are popping up more or less everywhere, movements of men who want to communicate and better understand their gender identity as males. And when they meet, a question emerges immediately: "How did we ever get into the state we're in?"

Origins of a Collapse

The fact is that during and after the Second World War, a process ended in the West (a process that began in the nineteenth century with the advent of industrialization in Europe) that triggered a sort of anthropological fracture between males and the previous masculine culture. For the past fifty years, and for the first time in the history of male human beings, males were no longer initiated into society and introduced into the world of adults by their fathers, or by male figures standing in for the father; now, for the first time, this rite of passage was supervised by the mother, and by a series of female figures (suffice it to mention the prevalence of women in the Western education system, in service industries, in psychology, and so on). This has led to an interruption in the transmission of male material and instinctive culture, which the mother could not possess

Klaus Kinski in *L'Important c'est d'aimer*, 1974, directed by Andrzej Zulawski

facing page: Takashi Murakami, *My Lonesome Cowboy*, 1998

Fiat Lingotto
factory,
department of
heavy hydraulic
presses, Turin,
1935

facing page:
Borsa di Tokyo,
1991.
Photo by Gordon

132

represents instead, and perfectly, the figure of the Great Mother, which is unfailingly active in the collective subconscious. In keeping with the style of that archetype, the corporation tends to find gratification by satisfying the needs of the consumer/children, and always seeks out greater and greater power. But, above all, it tends to create competition instead of solidarity among men (solidarity, on the other hand, has always typified masculine institutions: the army, the militia, or guilds and trade unions). Instead, the corporation tends to break the emotional and symbolic unity of men, pitching them against each other in competition to obtain the favors of the Great Mother/company.

A Weak Identity

The result of this interruption in the transmission of male material and instinctive culture, naturally, has been a weakening of the identity of males, for whom that culture is a fundamental component. Anthropology, biology, and philosophy all teach that the array of human instincts is weak to begin with. Man (not males alone, but

(since she belonged to a different gender) and therefore could not communicate even had she desired to (instinct cannot be learned from books: it must be experienced individually or in groups).

Since that shift, men have been like animals without noses: certainly, men have a brain, but they can't find their prey, they can't find their way back to their den, they can't find their mates.

The reasons behind this phenomenon are complex. For instance, during the war men remained far from home and family for many years; many never returned. Those who did make it back saw an epochal

transformation take place before their astonished eyes in the space of a few years: the triumph of the huge corporation, increasingly multinational.

The corporation is an institution that is by and large indifferent and, indeed, hostile to relationships of inheritance of skills and power through blood ties among its members, which—unlike the crafts workshop, or the old-fashioned farming cooperative, or even the traditional professional studio or office—tends to break up the relationship on the job between father and son. The corporation then goes on to absorb all of the energy of the male parent, leaving the mother and, above all, public or private institutions run by women to see to the education of boys. Moreover, a large corporation, wrongly presented as an expression of masculine psychology,

humanity at large) does not exist, but comes into existence, over the course of a difficult apprenticeship. That is why the transmission of "gender" is so important.

The human being, in fact, is the only animal that is born without knowing "instinctively" how to love, how to make love, how to fend for itself, and how to organize its own emotions and relationships. The psychoanalyst and anthropologist Alexander Mitscherlich points out that "men have no inherited model of behavior either for courtship or for mating, and their knowlege about how to recognize enemies is not inborn." In the past it was always the father who taught men to do these things, aided by a series of other figures, ranging from the master of arts and crafts to the teacher, the military instructor, and the sports instructor. Without this initiation, at some deep level, men did not feel like men. A weak identity gave rise to fears. This led to the accentuation of "infantile" behavioral traits that, according to the Dutch biologist Louis Bolk, increasingly typify the human condition; human beings are already somehow retarded, taking comparatively longer than other mammals to grow, to become self-sufficient, to break free.

The fading of the figure of the father/initiator has had profound consequences on the creativity and capacity for renewal of society at large. In the symbolic system of the collective subconscious, the father, in fact, represents the principle of action and the creation of new forms (including social forms), while the mother satisfies the needs for existing forms. The father is the "producer of the new," which the maternal figure and force will then nourish. This is why the weakening of the paternal figure—making man greedier and more calculating, more conservative and reluctant to contribute to social change—weakens society as a whole, making it less creative.

From Action to Need: The Great Mother Society

And, indeed, during the process that we have described here, culture (in its anthropological sense, a way of living) in the West has gradually fallen under the guidance of the female/maternal principle of the satisfaction of needs, with a consequential marginalization of the male principle of action, especially risky action. Risky behavior, besides reducing consumption (dead men don't consume), conflicts with the principle of "biopower," that is, the maintenance of life at all costs, noted by the philosopher Michel Foucault as one of the distinctive features of Western modernity.

Under the imperative of the "satisfaction of needs," conducive to the expansion of consumption and therefore the growth of industrial society, society has become a Great Mother, which has as its prime goal the maintenance of the individual and the satisfaction of his or her needs.

The satisfaction of needs, however, as a principle of social orientation leads in turn to the weakening of instinctive drives.

Contemporary Western society has wound up demonstrating what the anthropologist Arnold Gehlen (in his work on late cultures) called the risk of "excessive exoneration" from danger and effort. Seeing one's needs satisfied without effort or risk weakens the individual and prevents a sense of gratitude. For example, the preemptive satisfaction of need eliminates hunger, and produces anorexia, a typical condition of wealthy societies. Sex and the other forms of freedom nowadays distributed in "prepackaged" versions contribute to the phenomenon known among sexologists as the "decline of desire."

In fact, life develops and continues only when the male and female principles—man and woman—live in harmony and equilibrium. What is needed is both the male, creator of new forms through action, and the female, skillful conserver, with her receptivity, of the forms that already exist. Nowadays the prevalence of female values (specifically, the satisfaction of needs) and the simultaneous reduction of the paternal role, with ensuing impoverishment of male identity, are threatening the vital drive of Western society. When one or the other of these aspects is weakened, on either an individual or a collective level, the vital instinct is also threatened, along with desire and the capacity to live. The drive to reproduce is reduced; an increasing share of resources is destined to the elderly, who are no longer replaced by new "productive" individuals, and the overall array of resources diminishes. That is precisely the situation that we are witnessing today in the Western world.

Reaction for Survival and Change

All the same, the instinct for self-preservation reacts precisely when one reaches the lowest ebb. Thus, we see everywhere in the world a growing pursuit of research into "primordial forces," described by the anthropological movement of primordialism, which has observed on a planetary scale a renewed need for roots and relationships with the symbolic fathers of clans, tribes, and cultures, the original forerunners and masters. Along with this search for their symbolic ancestors, men who are committed to a new setting down of roots and a rebirth of their gender tend to seek out a relationship with the fundamental elements (not fabricated, but eternal) that are active in matter, but also in the human psyche: earth, water, fire, and air. It is in the context of this research that "men's movements," in the U.S. but also in Europe, go into the woods, to wild places, in search of a "strong" relationship with the primary natural elements, forces that have moved in their bodies and their souls from time immemorial.

The One Who Saves Himself: The Savage

In the context of these observations, but above all, with a view to reawakening these vital drives and emotions, men have begun a quest, nowadays, for the "savage man" within. This figure, the guiding image of men at the transition to the new millennium, is first and foremost an antidote, a poison killer, a countermeasure to the distancing from instinct produced by industrial society, in part through the fading role of the father. We should state immediately that this "savage" has nothing in common with the image of Rousseau's "noble savage," which never existed, historically or anthropologically, hovering between a mythical Eden and the authoritarian state that the creator of that image, Rousseau, inadvertently helped to create. As Freud immediately recognized, "it is not even worth talking" about the "noble savage" (precisely because of the lack of scientific foundation). The savage I am describing is "he who saves himself," to use the words of Leonardo da Vinci. He saves himself through his knowledge, at once natural and transcendent. Like the wise man of the woods, for instance, the *selvadego* cited in so many legends of the Italian Alps teaches natural lore to the peasants, such as how to make cheese and how to process the products of nature. An archetypal depiction of the savage can be seen in frescoes on the walls of many Alpine churches: he is the good barbarian, a Saint Christopher who carried the Infant Jesus on his shoulders across the river, helping him to go where he is unable to go alone.

The Conflict between Culture and Good Manners

The power of this archetype derives, nowadays, from the tension—noted by Thomas Mann as well—between two different aspects of human life.

On the one hand, Mann noted, there was *Kultur*, which corresponds to the style of the traditional material culture and the ways of everyday life, and with the values that underlie them. On the other hand, *Zivilisation*: the civilization of "good manners," artificial, of which the linguistic and behavioral masquerade of "political correctness" is probably the most up-to-date manifestation. Good manners scorn and shackle the instinctive drives as well as the development of the material and spiritual elements that make up *Kultur*: food, body, sex, relations with the primary natural elements (earth, air, fire, water), and their transcendent "counterparts," the archetypes or divine images, the most dynamic of which in the male field are king, warrior, wanderer, magician, and lover. And, of course, good manners are inimical to he who saves and liberates one and all, the savage.

Nearly all of the bloody wars of the last twenty years

Lou Ferrigno is the Incredible Hulk

facing page: Jayne Mansfield with her husband Mike Hargitay. Photo by Wayne Miller

have been triggered by an underestimation of the importance of traditional cultures (present in *Kultur*) of various peoples, in favor of abstract, intellectual, and political models. In all of these wars, the peoples that waged them did so in defense of their traditions, with their specific heritage of material and instinctive culture. This phenomenon, which—like that of the male— originates from a privation of identity, must be quickly understood, lest worse tragedies ensue.

Wilderness, or Unspoilt Nature

The man of the future will give an increasingly great priority to wilderness, or unspoilt nature, and the defense of a vital natural environment. Like all the most profound human experiences, its dynamic significance lies not in a "situation" (being in the wilderness) but in a relationship: to have a relationship with unspoilt nature, to have experienced an immersion in it, to have "felt" unspoilt nature. Therefore, it is not necessarily important how much there is (though, of course, in terms of instinctive organization, "the more wilderness there is, the better"), but rather the simple possibility of experiencing it. Here, too, then, it is not a matter of returning to an archaic "savage world," but rather a question of assisting in an environmental and territorial organization that will allow for this relationship with unspoilt nature.

We don't know what would happen in a world where wilderness vanished entirely, because such a phenomenon has never occurred in the history of the human race. All the same, from the observation of certain indications found in heavily urbanized areas with high population density, we may note the decline of certain primary vital drives. Among them are the desire and the capacity to reproduce, the capacity to defend oneself against an attack, and the decline of kindness and protectiveness toward the weaker and younger members of society.

A New Man for a New Era

As Ezra Pound, one of the century's great poets, knew perfectly well, the female is "better than man in 'useful gestures,' . . . but to man, given what [we] have of history, [is attributed] the 'inventions,' the new gestures, the extravagance, the wild shots, the impractical, . . . because in him the new up-jut."

But if the male becomes weaker, new actions, crazy ideas, tend to disappear, and without ideas, without the male drive, without the capacity for the gratuitous gift of phallic force, society can no longer renew itself, and will precipitate toward a crisis. That is why the new man—the male that has found in love an age-old capacity of giving to others and to the world, to other men, to women, to children, to society—will be the key figure in the transition to a new century and a new millennium.

Anthony Perkins
during a break
in the filming
of the film
On the Beach,
1959. Photo
by Wayne Miller

facing page:
Titian, *Saint
Christopher*.
Venice, Palazzo
Ducale

137

Uta Brandes

FROM HERE TO THERE: MALENESS AS A FLUCTUATING GENDER

Masculinity and Androgyny

Images like the following appear more and more frequently nowadays: on a poster or in a commercial, we see a person—more or less undressed—doing something. At first glance, we cannot catalogue this human being, we cannot quite see if it is a man or a woman, a boy or a girl. At times there are two characters, and normal perception would suggest that we are looking at a man and a woman. But we cannot be sure: what if it is a man with a man? Or a woman with a woman? Imagery that hints at the disappearance of explicit categories of gender is used (as a strategy) and accepted (as a form of consumption) in places where avant-garde products are created and sold, at the boundary between tomorrow and the day after tomorrow: in fashion, in the variegated field of accessories, in the fields of cosmetics and sports. Androgynous bodies, in all their ambiguity, are deployed to promote unisex fashion and beauty products such as cK One, Calvin Klein's eau de toilette for men and women. A further frontier is the blurring of gender categories in fashion, of which dresses for men is an extreme example.

Prompted by these observations, in this essay I shall set forth a thesis that may seem a bit daring (or even reckless), which the future will either prove or disprove. For the moment, at any rate, it exists as only a vague hypothesis, for it is not yet detectable even in the most radical trends of fashion.

Let us go far beyond the idea that specific genders (male or female) are shifting in favor of androgyny (with the presence of male and female attributes in the same person). In the future, a third possibility will arise, in the middle ground between "either one or the other" and the variant of "both one and the other": the variant of "neither one nor the other." Without a doubt, this is a far more complex condition. Just the idea of what it is that occupies this "middle ground" is immensely problematic. Western culture has developed in an increasingly sharply drawn distinction between opposites, in thought and practice, and this is particularly evident in regard to gender.

A human being must be either male or female and, according to this logic of evident alternation, each gender is given characteristics and attributes: "he" is identified, in order to be recognized and summoned. These definitions are so deeply embedded in our social and cultural systems that the constructions "masculine" and "feminine" are considered objective realities and therefore, in a certain sense, they became a sort of "social" nature.

Over the past thirty years, of course, the hard lines defining sexual identity have started to fade. The sharpness of distinctions, which made it possible to orient oneself in everyday life, is blurring. Cultural development engendered new modes for women (they can now be ambitious, tough, and daring, and so forth), which are counterbalanced by softer male qualities. These changes are transmitted first and foremost through physical images. As early as the Sixties, androgynous fashion models were becoming common, though they could still be identified as belonging to the female sex. Even the sharp-angled, extremely skinny Twiggy, who represented the prototype of the boy/woman, left no doubts about her gender: her huge eyes filled with wonder; her long slender legs were barely covered by an unquestionably feminine miniskirt. Male bodies meanwhile began to acquire attributes that were once the exclusive attributes of women: long hair, loose or in pony tails; full and sensual lips; a gaze that is not virile and determined, but infantile and full of wonder; movements that are often awkward; a request for

Transexual in Patong, Thailand, 1998. Photo by Fabio Polenghi

protection that probably arouses in women—along with sexual attraction—a certain maternal instinct. It is obvious that nowadays masculine physical images are no longer all of the same type. Numerous different models have been offered, going back to certain young men of the Sixties and early Seventies, with their lace-trimmed shirts worn over often startlingly skinny torsos.

(In the eighteenth century, the age of Rococo, males of the French aristocracy briefly adopted an even more feminized style: their sensibility and their willingness to abandon themselves to their feelings found expression in a joyous fashion, rich in lace, curls, flounced jackets, and floral patterns. Clean-shaven, scented, powdered, embellished, and, in some cases, adorned with fake beauty-marks, they explicitly tried to imitate *la femme*. For that matter, it was a time like today when women possessed power.)

And nowadays? If it was women who were the first,

facing page:
The winner of the Mr. America contest, Santa Monica, 1961: Ray Routledge, twenty seven, father of five children, Air Force sergeant. Measurements: 50 in. (chest), 32 in. (waist), and 18 in. (biceps)

Nomads, eastern
Mauritania, 1993.
Photo by
Franco Zecchin

in the Seventies, to rebel—in real life as well—against the role that had been historically assigned to them, now it is men who are abandoning their own position, considered until recently invulnerable.

Men are venturing into unknown territory, slipping into androgyny, openly declaring themselves homosexual or bisexual, undergoing sex changes, neglecting their careers in order to spend more time with home and family. It goes without saying that the picture I am drawing here describes only a minority of men, but we are looking for signs pointing to an unknown future. And aside from these spectacular indications of transformations that are directly visible, there is a broader paradigm shift underway in male existence. The typically masculine mentality, possessing firmness, determination, ambition, toughness, self-control, the drive for power, is beginning to disintegrate. What is emerging in its place is a surprising "in-between," an intermediate situation that is something more than an integration of "both-this-and-that." It is more than a sort of indeterminate gray space that attempts to make up for something that has been lost, and not merely a form of opportunism: a little of this and a little of that, so that nobody is disappointed or offended. It is not simply a general legitimization that forces no one to make a decision: I am not only this, but I am also that.

Instead, what is truly interesting and represents a genuinely new development is the unprecedentedly indeterminate nature of this intermediate space, which could be characterized as that of "neither one nor the other." In this case, the vagueness should be interpreted as a refusal, a negation. What is rejected is the obligation to decide between the two alternatives, male and female, and therefore to accept the bipolar counterpoint between the sexes; what is also rejected is the integration of feminine and masculine qualities.

In the future, this space could make room for a new self that would reject both the polarity of male/female and the integration of male/female. What would thus develop would be a self that would overwhelm all the categories and classifications heretofore applied.

This idea is still extremely vague, in part because our culture is so deeply rooted in oppositions: white or black, winner or loser, rich or poor, male or female. Other

cultures are not burdened with these inane absolutes.

A first example. The Inuit have more than twenty words in their language to indicate the color white. Since they live in an environment made up chiefly by a constant blanket of snow and ice, they have developed enormous perceptive skills in distinguishing among many subtle shades of white. The definition and distinction between this or that nuance, however, does not lead to the idea of characterizing the differences as contradictions. Through the use of language as a symbolic system, and thanks to shared understanding, social communication expresses even the slightest nuances. In other words: white is not a non-differentiated white, nor is it understood as the opposite of black or some other color, but neither is it a mixture of a dirty white or a gray; rather, it is something that we can described as many-hued. In fact, when we say that something is many-hued, we do not mean that we have mixed all colors into a single new color; rather we imagine many variegated colors coexisting one alongside the other, without defining any hue in particular.

A second example. Certain ancient African tribal cultures do not identify people in terms of two opposite genders. Rather, people are characterized in terms of an overall way of considering human beings: from the social context and from the way in which each individual forms his or her own array of behaviors, activities, and skills. It is almost impossible to translate, because here too, as with the Inuit, we are well beyond the parameters of our normal faculties of representation and language. Individuals that in our culture would be classified as men or women are defined variously as: man-man, woman-woman, man-woman, man-man-woman, woman-woman-man, woman-woman-woman-man, man-man-man-woman, and so on.

I have chosen these examples from other cultures because, transformed metaphorically into our own culture, they offer us an idea of how a neither-nor

Michael Gates,
Pretty Pony,
Sydney Gay
Parade.
Photo by
Penelope Clay.
Powerhouse
Museum, Sydney,
Australia

humanity might be configured in the future. Here we are referring to something specific that transcends contradiction and polarization (absolute genders), but also compromise and reconciliation (androgyny, hermaphrodism).

In this new setting, different relations would become possible that might sweep away all the patterns that are now familiar. Although there is no reconciliation in my model, the separation of genders would be eliminated. Since we are not accustomed to thinking in this manner and experience has not yet offered us images of this "neither/nor," it remains for now mysterious, undepicted, indistinct. This diverse depiction of difference and "otherness" would be a quality that might finally emerge directly from human beings, if there was sufficient courage to do more than present this innovation as a short-term trend but also to stabilize it within social contexts. If so, one problem would remain still unsolved: the relations "between" men and women.

facing page:
Moschino,
advertising
campaign for his
spring/summer
1989 women's
wear collection.
Photo by
Stefano Pandini

Alain Weill

VICISSITUDES OF AN INVENTORY

The Adventures of a Masculine Wardrobe

It has been more than ten years since I wrote (and published, at my own expense, in 1989) an inventory of my wardrobe.

This slightly kooky project finally saw the light thanks to a friend, a woman who has been a privileged observer of my sartorial adventures over the years; she offered

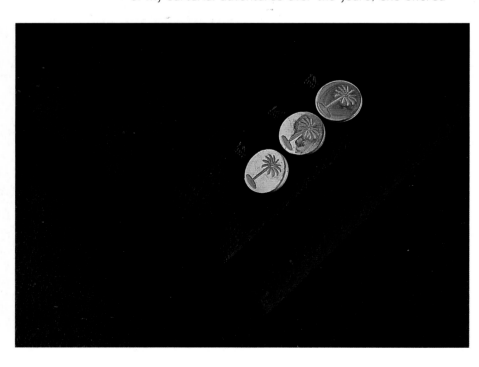

to write about the subject, and since there was no shortage of angles to explore and since over the past twenty years I had really devoted a considerable amount of time to that wardrobe, I ultimately decided it would be interesting to do the book—if for no other reason, as a form of exorcism.

I was the scion of a middle-class family that had never distinguished itself for its love of beauty; probably in reaction, as a teenager I became fascinated with clothing. The fathers of two of my friends had nearly attained the perfection of fashion plates. What most struck—and intrigued—me was the fact that, even though these two men were not particularly handsome, each and every day they constructed for themselves a new exterior of luxurious refinement. It began to become clear to me how it was possible to avoid passing unobserved through one's own personal effects. And since I had a sufficiently clear self-image to know that I was no Adonis, I decided to follow in their footsteps . . . in their elegant masculine footsteps, to be exact. It is a path full of treacherous pitfalls, requiring a lengthy apprenticeship, especially for those who do not possess unlimited funds.

A person can become quite depressed, after all, when—following painful and time-consuming economies—one finally purchases that exact pair of loafers and, after ten days of exquisite torture, it becomes clear that they will never quite fit. There is a genuine psychic torment involved in having a suit made, and seeing that there is a

this spread and
following pages:
Suits and
accessories from
the wardrobe of
Alain Weill.
Photos by
Ralph Delval

vague industrial cut to it, and knowing deep down that it will never really fit quite right. Well, one must be patient; *à la guerre comme à la guerre*: one must go on, one must purchase shirts, ties, fabrics, and one must go on seeking out new combinations of colors and patterns.

Considerable help came during the Seventies from a few select shopkeepers in New York City: there at least I could find suits in my exact size, that of a little German Jew who was (already!) becoming somewhat—aaah—broad in the beam.

With a little bit of extra money, I set out in Paris, as well, to find suppliers whose names nowadays are synonymous with an almost prohibitive luxury, but who at the time were still building their clientele, and who still could find it in their hearts to send fairly moderate, understated bills.

That is how I discovered an old shoemaker, almost seventy, who still had the humility to describe himself as "an apprentice of Niklitch," a tailor of the same age, who had a shop near the Madeleine, at the same address where, at the end of the nineteenth century, his grandfather had set up business after leaving England. Three generations later, the grandson still had working relationships with English manufacturers who supplied him

with fabrics in the colors he selected. This happiness lasted only a few years; age and ready-to-wear clothing soon swept these dinosaurs away.

And so I was forced to resume my quest, taking what I could find in various major *maisons* that took pity on me, until I discovered Hong Kong, a true paradise on earth: shelves stocked with old cloth imported from London, tailors from Shanghai stooped and practically ageless, shirtmakers who were never intimidated, no matter the pattern. Add to this the discovery of a young shoemaker willing to make shoes exclusively for (and with) me, and you will understand why, at the end of the ninth decade of the twentieth century, I had plenty of topics to discuss in that original little book.

One hundred forty-one shirts, 205 ties, 13 jackets, 45 suits, 31 pairs of shoes: the ark was definitely full! I had allowed myself every whim: juxtaposing various striped fabrics, all sorts of mixing and matching, diabolical zebra patterns.

If I had taken the whole thing seriously, that inventory might have represented my triumph, the apogee of my career, followed by the inevitable decline. Since I hardly took the thing as world-shaking (I dare say that the preface indicated my lighthearted approach), it was

a great source of amusement to me to notice the reactions of that microcosm of individuals who took interest in what was, after all, a semiclandestine work. The reaction of what I call patented dandies (that is, those miserable souls who believe that dandyism is primarily a matter of the tailor's tape measure) was a predictable outburst of envy and jealousy. One of them even began to spread the word that he owned more shoes than I did, and that his, moreover, had been made by better-known shoemakers. Another one took offense because I had even counted my T-shirts. From this point of view, I had a surprising confirmation of the fundamentally comic nature of the entire affair. A few curious readers, happily, perfectly grasped the sense of irony with which I had approached the entire enterprise.

Although it failed to cure me entirely, the little book I published did encourage me in the course of the retreat I was undertaking day by day in terms of look and appearance. The quality of a well-cut suit, a pair of shoes that fit well—these are precious, solitary pleasures that can only be given one name: comfort. Today comfort is the focus of my concerns, and I can reasonably take that as a sign of maturity.

Men's fashion, too, with its famous labels and names, has undergone considerable evolution, and the array it offers now is incomparably greater than that of my younger years. Nowadays, you can find practically all possible colors, materials, cuts, and sizes, while genuine custom-made clothing is virtually priceless: perhaps it should be classed as one of the habits destined to disappear; after all, that is how societies evolve.

If I was going to redo an inventory of my wardrobe, the result would be much different, but I have no such intention. What we are most often given these days is the freedom to play with shapes, forms, styles, and colors. If a man chooses not to, he can simply wear a gray suit and a fine silk tie with a prancing-horse pattern. I personally cannot forget that when I was a boy, white-collar workers wore jackets that did not match their trousers, which were threadbare and shapeless at the knees and in the seat. Perhaps, in those days, that was what most frightened me. Today, there is no reason for anyone to fear such a fate. "Being" means so much more, and "appearing" has lost much of its meaning. All that remains is an enjoyable esthetic game: a few minutes in which to begin the day with a bit of brio by choosing the right outfit. Which is how I try to preserve myself, relying upon the relics of a glorious past.

Natalia Aspesi

MILITARY STYLE

The Reappearance of Uniforms in the Icon of Masculinity

The icon of man in war has become tragically relevant because of the fighting in the former Yugoslavia. The uniforms that we see on television are no longer parade uniforms, elegant, martial, with lots of glittering gilt medals and badges. Instead, we see combat uniforms, heavy, clumsy, which force the men who wear them to move awkwardly and dangerously: camouflage pants and shirts, bulletproof vests with lots of pockets and pouches, utility belts that crisscross the body, festooned with canteens and pistols, submachine guns on straps for easy aiming, first-aid kits, knapsacks, hand grenades and other munitions, and on the head, a helmet made of some high-tech material, almost always worn askew and unbuckled, just like in war movies.

Even though women are now enlisted in the armies of many nations, and even go into combat, war remains the most virile of events, requiring the virtues that have traditionally been considered primarily masculine: courage, daring, altruism, and self-sacrifice. War tends to transform death (the everyday indispensable ingredient of increasingly savage fiction and film, a factor that has lost its sense of fatality through our increasingly imaginary and superficial contact with life) into the supreme and sublime act of heroism, elevated high above the anonymous heartbreaking deaths of masses, of entire populations, lamented and forgotten in the space of a news cycle. Thus, men at war move us far away from everything that sociologists, anthropologists, and sexologists have said

about the man of today, on the subject of which (just like the subject of the woman of today) studies, surveys, and research pours out in floods, often with alarming conclusions, and even more often with absurd ones. If there is a war, if men are called to fight, to risk their lives, to drop bombs or kill other men, or even to take part in humanitarian actions, or police actions, or pacifications, then it becomes totally pointless to speculate whether the contemporary male is fragile or vain, whether he fears women or is increasingly discovering that he is bisexual or homosexual, whether he is impotent or excessively horny, whether he is more or less intelligent, more or less aggressive, more or less independent than the woman of today. Or, further, whether he is depressed or lonely, if he wants to move in a herd or if he is a fashion victim, if he fears the future or abhors the politicization of life, whether he is liberal or conservative. War is an elemental tragedy that places all men on the same level, relieving them of all individual, social, or personal problems, making them all members of the masses, deleting features and even their membership in this tribe or that.

It is no accident that uniforms are called "uniforms": and while real experts who see military footage on

Chelsea pensioners, Royal Hospital, London, 1998. Photo by John Londei, London

television can immediately tell by the type of camouflage (large spots, small ones, speckles, tiger stripes, patchy) on the uniforms, or the number of pockets on the trousers, by the weapons, and, in some cases, even by the kind of ski mask covering the face, whether they are American or British soldiers, French or Italian, many of us—who might have little difficulty in distinguishing an Armani jacket from a Prada—cannot say from the pictures we see on television whether we are looking at a NATO soldier or a member of the Serbian army. Television, moreover, shows a particular type of war, as ordered by military commanders: unreal, clean, where blood and massacre seems to visit only civilians, or occasionally enemy soldiers, never "our" men.

We know, Mr Weller—we who are men of the world—that a good uniform must work its way with the women, sooner or later.
—Charles Dickens, *Pickwick Papers*

Only one movie in recent memory has shown us the horror, the slaughter, the blood and guts, the terror and noise of battle, and that is *Saving Private Ryan*, considered by many to be almost unwatchable in its ferocious realism. But it was only a movie, and moreover a movie about a long-ago war, the Second World War. The odd thing about war today (the war in the Balkans, certainly not the other wars, generally ignored, that are creating bloodbaths in Guinea-Bissau, Kashmir, Angola, between Ethiopia and Eritrea, in the Congo) is that, to judge from the images that we see at home, the uniforms don't even get dusty, much less dirty. It is a conflict where soldiers never seem to die, only civilians, and in considerable number. It is a war of concealment and lies, where television and newspapers say only what is permitted by military commanders.

There were centuries when hundreds of thousands of men spent their (short) lives at war; for many, that was the only work available, the only way to survive. To work as a mercenary in the service of one despot or another was a desirable and well-paid profession, which allowed the victorious army to engage in looting, rape, and the raw exercise of power. Even in peacetime, which tended to be brief, important men would have their portraits painted in uniform, a mark of supreme power. Girls used to fall in love with young officers in their tight-fitting uniforms, while medals and gold braid made older men irresistible. A man in a uniform, one of the handsome uniforms of the past, emanated all of the allure of virility in its strongest and most heroic moment. Who can imagine Napoleon or Nelson, Victor Emmanuel II or Francis Joseph I in anything but a uniform, perhaps a dress uniform, loaded down with ribbons and plumage?

The time of the greatest splendor of military uniforms was the seventeenth century, when colorful, brightly caparisoned troops met in fields and fought bloody battles. At a certain point, in Italy, officers became so exhibitionistic and recherché that it became necessary to issue decrees against excessive luxury. In 1779, for instance, a regulation forbade the ornamentation

Fighting Load

86

of uniforms, specifically with precious stones and jewels on shoe buckles, or artificial flowers on hats, excessively garish ribbons on one's ponytail, or too much lace in one's sleeve. The various colors identified not only membership in a certain regiment, but also allegiance to a certain nation, making it easy to see the enemy. If not the uniform, then at the very least a cockade on the hat indicated, with its color, whether the owner belonged to the Piedmontese army (light blue), the French army (white), the Spanish army (red), or the imperial army (black). This was the time of what were known as "the lace wars," because of the dainty luxury of certain uniforms, even on the battlefield. For instance, white was the favorite color for uniforms, an absurd color because of its visibility and because it was inevitably destined to be splattered with blood and dirt. White was the color of the uniform jackets of the Prussian dragoons and their Belgian counterparts, white was the color of the leggings of the grenadiers of Saxony and of the Russian infantry, white was the color of the breeches of the Savoy light troops and of the Belgian volunteers, while the uniform of the infantry of the empress of Austria, Marie-Therese, was entirely white, embellished by red or dark blue borders, broad sashes and golden tassels, silver buttons, equally white transverse stripes, a three-cornered hat edged in white, dainty black shoes.

On the battlefield, the luxurious elegance of hussars and noble guard gave an indication of the power of an

Existence Load

87

flaunting of expensive and spectacular uniforms, nowadays only small insignia on the collar or sleeve, often nearly invisible on the camouflaged material, separate General Clark from the unknown, anonymous private. It is an invisibility that is necessary to war, which cancels not only the hierarchic scale, but above all the person.

In places that enjoy peace, in a world where there are no tragedies of dictatorship and war, men—and not just young men—take endless pains over their bodies, their muscles, their appearance, which they dream of making athletic: they work out and play sports, they have massages, they oil themselves, rid themselves of body hair, obsess over a certain satiny physicality that they pursue by all means possible, driven by the images they have seen in print ads and television spots that flaunt male beauty, its cold commercial carnality, its mass-market reliance on youth. Then an army imposes a uniform on these same young men, and their bodies disappear, they become standardized, like all the others; they are changed from objects to be admired, embellished, and protected into a different object, exposed, threatened, canceled. The memoryless young man immersed in marketed superficiality is suddenly asked to rediscover the ancient virtues of his species and his gender, virtues that have been entirely eliminated by the needs of a global marketplace that does not call for heroism, daring, the spirit of sacrifice, but instead pursues and seduces with its hedonistic and sexual lures.

And yet war with all its horrors and combat uniforms with all their menace remain as a mirage of strength and masculinity at the bottom of the hearts of many men who, to their good fortune, have never experienced war. Successful magazines are published that report each month on the wars of the world and the new American smart bombs (laser-guided, TV-guided, GPS-guided). There are videocassettes with reconstructions of famous air or naval battles. There are plenty of lavish and expensive books on the uniforms of every regiment and army imaginable from antiquity to the present day (in America especially, massive tomes with stunning illustrations and names like *Camouflage Uniforms of the Waffen SS*, or *Tigerstripe Combat Fatigue Uniforms of the Vietnam War* are published). It may be some consolation to know that these scholarly books dedicated to men at war are not necessarily purchased by war-mongering maniacs, but often by fashion designers. There is not an ankle boot, a pocket, a turned-up shirtsleeve, shoulder bag, belt, beret, overalls, T-shirt, or knapsack—all items that have featured prominently in the mass fashions of the past few years—that wasn't copied from these savage souvenirs of the killing fields, proof once again of how a people at peace can forget the true meaning of war.

151

"Care and use of individual clothing and equipment," *U.S. Army Field Manual*, 1977

army, of the nation that had equipped and armed it. In *The Emperor and the Assassin*, the latest magnificent film from the Chinese director Chen Kaige, there is a particularly impressive scene that gives an absolute sense of an unstoppable power and a certain victory, even before the battle is joined. A fierce band of rebels enters the great courtyard of the palace of the future emperor (the film is set in the third century B.C.). The emperor appears, dressed in white, at the top of a giant staircase; alone and apparently defenseless, he looks at the rebel horde and withdraws as if defeated. Then, without warning, dozens of identical gates all open at once, and from each a powerful warrior emerges. Endless lines of men advance, thousands and thousands of men (the film uses 300,000 extras), all carrying the same spears, holding the same shields, wearing the same stone-gray clothing. The men disappear into an absolute and homogeneous entity, an armed body, an army. After so many centuries, the army still shows this capacity for standardization, transformation of many individuals into a whole of a radically different nature. A threat, a mass deliverer of death, whose component members must be ready and willing to die.

One characteristic of the wars of today is that camouflage uniforms make it difficult to tell soldiers of not only different armies apart but also different ranks within the same army. If colonels, generals, and captains could once be told from the enlisted men by their proud

*Artist Rifle
Series*, 1997,
multiple self-
portrait.
Photos by Paul
M. Smith

Photographs by Stefano Torrione

KOKBORU

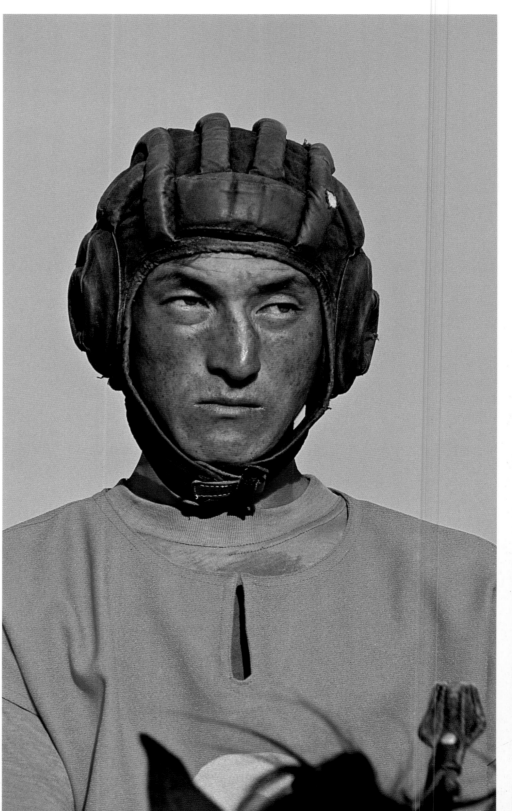

National
championship
of "kokboru,"
an ancient game
of Kyrgyzstan.
Bishkek,
Kyrgyzstan,
1999.
Photos by Stefano
Torrione

David Le Breton

ATHLETIC ORDEALS

Extreme Sports, Heroism, and Virility

162

A Passion for Risk

Risk entails uncertainty. In extreme sports, the thrill of action is counterbalanced by the likelihood of disaster or failure. When an expert mountain climber tells us that, from his point of view, crossing the street in a major city is more dangerous than climbing a mountain, he is really confirming that risk is always a subjective perception. Some risks exist almost completely in the realm of the imagination: only a very few have the courage to jump off a bridge with an elastic rope tied around their ankles, even though bungee jumping is relatively safe. Indeed, a pedestrian crossing a busy street in a big city runs a greater risk of dying or being injured. Of course, if they tried it, most people would experience disproportional fear at the moment they jumped and an equally outsize feeling of joy and inner strength upon returning to solid ground. If the person who is jumping is a professional, the evaluation of the risk is more objective, but such situations are never truly neutral, nor are the attraction and allure that they exert.

In the case of extreme physical challenges, risk is always present, even if it is limited by skill and intuition. Death is held off at a respectful distance: it is addressed more than actually wrestled with, even though—from time to time—it bursts onto the scene, just to remind everybody of the one limit that cannot be surpassed, and injury is common. Who among us is not moved by

Viva Knievel,
1976, directed by
Gordon Douglas

stories of overcoming great adversity? Eric Dumont, a journalist who is hard at work on a hagiography of the postmodern hero, strikes a familiar chord: "Those daring men that I have met play dice with their lives . . . seeking tirelessly to achieve the impossible; they walk upon the waters of the oceans, they fly around the world, they climb the highest peaks without oxygen tanks, they work on the bottom of the seas, they live on wind. They run, they sail, they fly, and they dream with greater intensity, faster, farther, and higher than anyone in recorded history. They continually risk their lives. They are all dancing on the brink of the abyss." This dance on the razor's edge has by now pervaded everyday speech, and everyone talks about "daring," "challenges," "limits"— all terms that have become clichés.

A remarkable passion for risk has developed in Western societies at the end of the millennium. Traditional sources of meaning and value have lost their legitimacy—or perhaps we should say that they have lost

their general power—ceding greater autonomy to individuals. No one depends any longer on unambiguous moral codes or ideologies. In our increasingly individualistic societies, we seek to determine personal values by which to live. Each one of us can only offer an exquisitely personal response when questioned about the meaning and value of life. For some, the answer lies in subjecting themselves to physical tests. This is especially true of men, who are raised to express themselves through action and personal initiative. By taking on the world, one-on-one, and putting in play all of one's physical resources, extreme sportsmen can find the points of reference that are indispensable to the production of a personal identity. "To reach the end of one's rope," "to prove oneself," "to challenge oneself": these clichés inevitably carry a charge of meaning. The paradox of the extreme is that by focusing the body, one heals a dismembered sense of self. Everybody wants to feel alive (it may be the only way to be certain that we exist). Intense physical challenge is a way of "experiencing" a sense of unity and wholeness. Physical contact with the world brings the reassurance of the "limits" that are indispensable to existence.

The passion for the "limit" makes it possible to define one's own boundaries, to finally feel contained and supported. Brutal contact with the world replaces the filtered contact that takes place on the symbolic plane and provides a surer grip on one's own existence. Ivano Gagliardo, a young skater in Lausanne, who loves to skate at top speed in the middle of traffic, along the roads that run down to the lake, explains: "I need to know my exact worth, where I fit, each time. I am good at skating, why couldn't I be good at something else? I know how to do something . . . I forget all my troubles. There are lots of things to think about: my grip on the downhill stretches, speed, automobiles, pedestrians, the cops . . . I forget everything else." Ivano is well aware of the risks he is taking: "You could be run over by a car. You can be arrested. You can hit a pedestrian. But if you are good, if you are a master of the road, then racing reassures you, makes you stronger. You need to know that it is possible to run some risks and that, each time, you can overcome them." The lack of control over the world leads to a desire for intense physical immersion that is limited, temporary, in which an individual can affirm a sovereignty that no one can question.

"When my heart is pounding loudly in my chest, I find out just how far I can go beyond the reasonable:

once the race is over, I truly know who I am," explains James Fixx, the man who popularized jogging in the United States. In order to experience this sense of intimate transfiguration, it is necessary to break from the tranquillity of everyday life via proximity to danger or the exhaustion of one's physical resources.

The Ordeal

In most physical and athletic activities, "limits" are not fixed (as we know from the fact that records are made to be broken). In extreme sports, however, practice is pushed to the limits of caution and skill. Some adventurers seek out death and challenge death in its own territory. This quest is reminiscent of the ordeal, a ritual form of trial in which the death of the accused was interpreted as evidence of his guilt, while his survival established his innocence. Trial by ordeal was practiced in the West up to the Middle Ages and in other cultures as well. In the absence of tangible evidence that someone who had been accused of a grave crime was either innocent or guilty, society would call upon God (or the gods) to issue a verdict. If the accused survived a painful and dangerous ordeal, it proved that the deity was on his or her side in the declaration of innocence; if not, there was no longer any doubt in the community about his or her guilt. The vindicated subject acquired a renewed and even more solid position within the community. The supernatural power that had been invoked could not shirk its duties, but always gave a clear and unquestionable answer when petitioned by the community.

In present-day Western societies, the ordeal is a metaphor for a quest for truth relating to something greater than or outside of society. The gods have long departed, and instead we have cultures grounded in individualism undergoing crises of meaning. A modern ordeal is not sure what it is pursuing: it places in jeopardy the future of an individual who has lost the feeling of belonging to a society and delivers a verdict that concerns him and him alone. It has become transmogrified from a judicial procedure into an extreme rite of passage, a visit, as it were, to an oracle for deeply private consultation.

A modern ordeal challenges death to guarantee a form of self-worth. If the individual escapes the danger to which he has exposed himself, he is rewarded with proof that his life has meaning and value. In spite of our frequent assumption to the contrary, there is no suicidal component to facing extreme challenges. It is not a self-destructive form of behavior, precisely because it does not seek death, but life. The greater the risk, the greater is the reward: "The moment of survival is the moment of power," wrote Elias Canetti.

Alcuni uomini hanno cambiato il nostro modo di vivere, altri quello di sognare.

Questa sera **Italia 1** alle ore 22.50 dedicherà uno special in memoria di
Patrick De Gayardon.

facing page: Swedish gymnastics team, Florida, 1955

165

The Rewards of Risk

Risk taking, which most modern institutions are designed to minimize, awakens—or reawakens—the joy of living. For some, it is a way to regain control over a life that has fallen into doubt or chaos. In general, risk taking in extreme physical endeavor is a phenomenon that tends to attract individuals who are socially well integrated, who are trying to break out of a routine and escape the security of a well-oiled life. The quest for risk feeds the soul with an intensity that is otherwise missing. For such people, the sensations that are produced are all the more stimulating, as the rest of existence is peaceful, tranquil, and safe from surprises: note the sociological features that distinguish the members of a mountaineering club in California: "A typical member . . . is a white male aged about thirty-eight. He has been married for nine years and has one child. He has a graduate degree and works in some sector of the applied sciences; usually he is an electronic engineer or else an aerospace engineer. . . . He comes from a stable background, he enjoys a certain economic security, he is well educated, and he has a prestigious job." You need money and time to risk your life on a mountainside. For that reason, such pursuits are usually the domain of the middle-class and the privileged.

Fitness fair,
Rimini, 1995.
Photo by
Armin Linke

Those who practice the new sports whose chief attraction consists of risk or physical challenge explain the sense of jubilation that they feel at a moment of extreme stress with a recurring term: "explosion." Consciousness is lost or slackens momentarily in the paroxysm of a controlled mental infarction. The image of death is metaphorically conjured up by this enthusiastic phrase: it makes one think of a bomb going off inside the body. But the sensation of omnipotence is so powerful that the competitor emerges unharmed from the ordeal. An individual, thus rendered open or available, has the sensation of being penetrated, but not annihilated, by the world. The limits of the self expand, and the sense of joy is directly proportional to the risk of dying. François Cirotteau launches himself in a kayak from a waterfall twenty-eight meters high: "Careful: here, like in skiing or solo free climbing, the slightest error can cost you your life or put you in a wheelchair. The temptation to try this can be fatal." C. Taillefer, an adept at speed biking, races down snowy slopes at just under 170 kilometers per hour. "It's like flying," he explains. "If anything were to go wrong, there would be no time to react. The only thing you think before setting off is to remember to brake after the timed stretch."

"For me," says skier Jean-Marc Boivin, "what counts in particular is the idea of risk. If there is no risk, then there is really no sense of fun. . . . I feel sure that a certain element of uncertainty is indispensable. . . . In my efforts to set altitude records or records in extreme skiing, I don't like being too certain about the outcome, or feeling that everything has been too well prepared. It is too easy, if you know the terrain perfectly! Sometimes, before I set out on a very difficult challenge, I don't even know whether or not I am going to participate. I decide at the last moment, as if it was a reckless impulse." A little later in the same book Boivin explains, "In certain curves, you can stay on the course only by jamming down a ski pole, it is as if you were suspended in midair. Let there be even the slightest sheet of ice hidden beneath the mantle of snow, and it's over! Straight down you go! I find that to be particularly stimulating." At the start of the Vendée Globe Challenge in 1992—which would result in the death of a number of sailors—L. Perron told a journalist that "the Globe Challenge is like a giant arena into which fifteen modern gladiators enter. Everybody knows that in combat, someone is risking their life."

Look into the mind of Guy Delage, who crossed the Atlantic once on an ultralight plane and once by swimming. "Death, to me, is a magnetic attractor. . . . I have learned to live side by side with death, to look it in the eye, and quite often I have included it as a possibility to be considered in my plans. Certainly, there is the fun of risk. . . . I like to graze death without waiting around for it to get me: this subtle game gives me an immense pleasure. The continual sight of the one we must flee pumps waves of adrenaline through my veins . . . which is the source of the pleasure." Before diving off the coast of the Cape Verde Islands in an attempt to swim to the opposite coast of the Atlantic Ocean, Delage sent a number of postcards to his friends, writing: "Will the Atlantic let itself be crossed this time? If not, my friends

will receive this historic piece of paper bearing my fondest thoughts of them." Delage insists that there is no suicidal impulse driving him. "I am tremendously in love with life. I want to explore every nook and cranny of life, every possibility. I am simply trying to change the environment that envelops me, transforming it like a soap bubble, testing the envelope just short of making it pop. The game consists of grazing the breaking point, without making it pop. My experiences, extraordinary as they are, allow me to lead a life of intense passions."

"When I succeed in a challenge that is so close to

the edge, one of those experiences that make people say to me, 'It's just surprising that you are still alive,' for me it seems like a victory over death, a triumph over the dust that awaits us all, as well as a tribute to the two or three friends who die every year in the mountains," says Boivin, who met his death in 1989 in an accident in Venezuela. Risking death constitutes for some a way of life. In certain circumstances, the experience produces a new sense of identity. It may instill an intoxicating sensation of invulnerability.

For an instant, the well-trained and highly skilled

expert exchanges the certain for the uncertain, and the reward he is seeking is directly proportional to the risk he undertakes.

The Agony and the Ecstasy

When one attempts to "discover one's own limits" (as the cliché goes), the human body becomes the adversary, more or less obstinate, that must be conquered and forced to pay the price of performance.

In a fierce and closely fought battle, one comes into conflict with one's own flesh, knowing that the more one is marked by suffering at the finish line, the more significant and impressive the final outcome will be. Passing through physical pain proves the commitment of the competitor. Upon setting out to swim the Atlantic, Delage declared: "I want to experience pain, having experienced terror while flying an ultralight over the Atlantic." A French marathon racer expressed regret that he was unable to withstand pain for a longer time:

"Even though I am capable of facing pain," he said, "I am still not able to take the pain during training the way that I can during a race. . . . At the finish line of certain marathons, I have seen runners on their knees, in agony, people that take three days to get over it. For me, half an hour later, it is all over. I am still not able to get inside myself, to hurt myself. Maybe I am just simplifying things. It is something to work on, an apprenticeship." Pascal Pich, a policeman who claims that he is "seeking out the limits of the human body," has set a record of finishing thirteen triathlons in a row, swimming 49.5 kilometers, bicycling 2,430 kilometers, and running 549 kilometers: "What with tendinitis and periostitis of my left ankle and a cyst on my right knee, I try not to zigzag but to follow a straight line along the asphalt. Going straight is the most difficult thing to do," he declares after ten days of torturous exertion, broken only by daily three-hour intervals to eat and sleep. Just a short while before, he had fallen asleep on his bicycle, falling and hurting himself. In the pool, he had slammed against the side after falling asleep. "The engine that drives me," writes one stalwart kayaker, "is not my muscles, but my determination, my hatred of the discomfort that must be battled day after day, hour after hour, oarstroke after oarstroke, even though each successive one is more painful than the one that preceded it. I am a member of the resistance, in a war that I invented for myself. The enemy is also me, with all my physical weaknesses, with my desire to give up entirely." Giorgio Passino has been an Alpine guide for about thirty years, and is a passionate fan of extreme skiing and climbing up frozen waterfalls. A journalist provides us with a brief version of his medical history: "Over the course of his career, Passino has had several dozen accidents. He has broken just about everything: skull, shoulder, legs, fingers, hands, teeth. The most serious accident was in 1987: he wound up in the hospital with his right leg paralyzed. Seven fractures. 'Accidents never stopped me,' he says. 'Once I am back on my feet, I always return to my mountains!'"

Road races, half marathons, marathons, trekking—all are physical activities that offer the possibility of forging character, challenges that the protagonist never seems embarrassed to discuss: "I really went through everything imaginable," "It was terrible, but I would definitely do it again," "It wrings you dry, it wears you out completely." The word *tough* especially captures the feeling of mastering material that is unyielding. A surfeit of pain barely tolerated is transformed into pleasure, and one turns back to gaze with admiration on the trial endured.

Alongside personal pain, there is an image of becoming one with nature itself. The flesh of the world merges with the flesh of the body while, at the same time, remaining separate. "It is over," writes Jean-Louis Etienne. "I reach the North Pole skiing in a dream. It beckons to me, summoning me, and tears of fatigue burn in my eyes, but what happiness! It is an unparalleled night, on the brink of ecstasy, heavenly." For four days, Carla Perroti crossed the highest salt basin on earth, the Salar de Uyuni in Bolivia. By day, it is a furnace, at night, it is freezing, the sunlight is blinding,

and the air burns her throat. "I feel free," she says, "just like what I experienced in the Sahara. I have understood something truly essential. Allow oneself to be penetrated, do not attempt to resist. It is not human beings like us who establish the rules. . . . Every day, at the top of my lungs, I thank the Salar for having helped me to achieve my dream."

To be sure, the man of "me, me" may feel at the moment of a supreme test that he is immersed in the cosmos, but there is no doubt that he will be going back to his "me, me," to the normality of everyday life, in the course of a few days, with a full schedule beginning immediately after his return from the challenge.

Bungee jumping. Photo by Nathan Bilow/ Allsport USA

facing page: *Grosse Pyramide*, twenty-seven police sergeants on four motorcycles, performance by the German police at the Olympic stadium in Berlin, 1955

Alix Sharkey

NEW MEDIA, NEW MEN

The Lost Paradigm of Male Normality

The popular image of masculinity in Britain is largely defined by our men's magazines. A decade ago, I would have had to qualify that statement in terms of hetero- and homosexual definitions of masculinity, because of the difference between their respective representations of the male body. But over the last decade, advertising, which is always concerned with seduction, with creating verisimilitudes of freedom, has gradually undermined the white heterosexual male's defensiveness and persuaded him to shine like his homosexual counterpart.

As cultural theorist Mark Simpson states in *Male Impersonators: Men Performing Masculinity*, "Gay men, like blacks, as an 'extravagant' minority on the margins of society, had long provided a rich supply of fashions for capitalism to appropriate and bring into the mainstream. But in the 1980s straight men were no longer being sold just disco or cologne: instead the whole package was being promoted—the queer lifestyle, the individual young man indulging his desires outside the heterosexual family . . . narcissistic, sexy, single young men happy to throw their clothes off for the camera became the advertising ideal."

Of course, as Simpson points out, this selling of an overtly queer relationship with the male body has traditionally been framed in such a way as to blur the object of desire, in order to reassure those straight men buying into homoeroticism of the deeply heterosexual nature of their choice. After all, when our committed heterosexual consumer regards the perfectly toned and tanned bodies of other men in TV and magazine commercials, he is not gazing lovingly at another man; he is looking at an idealized version of himself. And when he looks back at the mirror and sees the imperfection of his own mortal condition, this spurs him to go out and buy the products that will bridge the gap between the two versions. Clearly, then, it would be outrageous to suggest that he might also get some kind of sexual thrill, albeit subliminal, from looking at these other male bodies.

To ensure that there can be no doubt about this, British men's magazines are increasingly full of photographs of seminaked young women. This trend was established shortly after, and in my opinion in direct response to, the 1980s advertising trend for objectification of the male body. In 1990 *Arena*, then the market leader, became the first British men's fashion magazine to feature a woman on its cover, with a relatively demure shot of "supermodel" Tatjana Patitz. It was a daring move, because at that time the nascent British men's magazine market was desperate to distinguish itself from "top shelf" soft-core pornographic magazines like *Playboy* and *Penthouse* (so called because porn mags are traditionally kept on a news agent's top shelf, that is, out of the reach of minors).

The floodgates were opened. Within months, all of the main men's titles were featuring top models and

Jeep advertising
campaign, 1999

Hollywood actresses on their covers. And then came *Loaded*. Billing itself as the magazine "for men who should know better," *Loaded* broke with tradition and tore up the rule book. Instead of pushing the aspirational values of *Arena*, *GQ*, and *Esquire*, it went in search of a new market and struck gold.

While the other magazines presented an image of masculinity that was supposedly urbane, witty, and well heeled, *Loaded* talked to its readers in their own idiom. If your typical *Arena* reader was an architect or a designer with an interest in vintage sports cars, minimalist hotel design, and a reverence for a well-made martini, *Loaded* made no pretense about its decidedly low-rent view of the world: blokes were blokes, they liked football, birds, and beer, and maybe a little bit of nose candy on a Saturday night. They had beer bellies, cracked dirty jokes, liked pornography, ate bacon sandwiches for breakfast, and only wore posh clothes for a big night out. Instead of supermodels, the covers of *Loaded* were dedicated to soap actresses, trashy pop singers, and TV presenters, with the odd porn star usually wearing a bikini or lingerie. Almost overnight it became the market leader, with a monthly circulation of 150,000, outselling its astonished rivals by almost two to one.

Since then, every new player to arrive at the table has simply upped the ante by including more tits and fewer long words. *FHM*, the trade said, was *Loaded*

with a frontal lobotomy. Whatever its faults, *Loaded* at least had a sense of humor. But *FHM* seemed to think its readers might not understand jokes if they were written down, so rather than embarrass them, it spoke very slowly and in monosyllables wherever possible. It also told them exactly how to do everything, from choosing a simple pair of jeans to ordering a meal. It was a how-to manual for the social Neanderthal, a magazine for men who couldn't read without moving their lips.

And this was its genius: it looked at *Loaded* and (who would have dreamed it was even possible?) decided to go down-market. It stole *Loaded*'s wide-boy swagger and dumbed it down—took out all the jokes, gave every T-shirt a star rating for quality and value, inserted the addresses of all the shops that sold it and the number of the bus you had to take in order to get there. Quite simply, it was an insult to anyone who could tie their shoelaces and whistle at the same time.

Naturally, it blew the competition out of the water. Within a couple of years it was the market leader, and remains so, with a circulation in excess of 750,000 copies a month.

Its success has not only spawned several imitators, but shifted the entire market's center of gravity. All British men's magazines now feature scantily clad women on their covers, and on several of their editorial pages, because it is now an article of faith in the

DAS MUSS GEKÜHLT WERDEN.

Astra. Was dagegen?

publishing industry that the success of men's magazines is in direct proportion to their nipple count. New arrivals like *Maxim* and *Front* are even more aggressive in their use of soft-core imagery. In fact, in a recent newspaper article, *FHM*'s editor was forced to admit that "*Front* makes *FHM* look like the genteel end of the market. It's a top shelf magazine for fourteen-year-olds." The irony of this statement will not be lost on anyone who has ever flicked through *FHM* in search of articulate, well-informed, adult opinion.

In 1998 *Maxim*, which has a circulation of 300,000 in the U.K., launched an American version, complete with typical feature articles: "Strip Club Secrets—Confessions of a Strip Club Bouncer" and a "lingerie runway" photo-spread of semiclad women, supposedly advising readers on what underwear to buy for their partners on Valentine's Day. Within a year it was the American publishing success of the decade, with eight hundred thousand readers.

This success has emboldened British men's magazines to the point where they are now openly flirting with pornography in ways that would have been unthinkable even ten years ago. And the remarkable financial success of these magazines has led other areas of the media to follow suit. Newspapers, women's and specialist magazines, TV, advertising, and, of course, the Internet are all increasingly loaded with soft-core imagery. As William Leith noted recently in the

Observer, soft-core pornography is now "beginning to seem normal in Britain. . . . Porn leads to more porn, better porn, more widespread porn, more pornographic porn. Porn becoming normalized. A cover line in this month's *Cosmopolitan* is 'make your own sexy video.' Soon, we will all be consumers of pornography. Not much later, we will start to produce it."

Even Dylan Jones, the former editor of *Arena* responsible for that 1990 cover that unleashed the publishing genre now known as the "New Lad" market, and now editor of *GQ*, laments the "puerile dementia that affects certain parts of the men's market," adding that "some of these magazines are little but how-to manuals for the faint of heart and mighty of wrist." However, his remarks should be seen in context: namely, an extended justification on the *Guardian*'s media pages for more of the same. Or, as he puts it, "*GQ* will feature women in its pages as it's vitally important that the magazine retains its libido."

What all this naked female flesh seems to indicate, however, is a deep crack in the heterosexual British male's self-image. For all their rampant flaunting of macho attitudes, and the supposedly ironic postures which accompany them, men's magazines are desperately trying to mask the poverty of contemporary masculinity. It's as if, knowing that some kind of radical curfew is just around the corner, they are indulging in one last binge of political incorrectness, one last mad

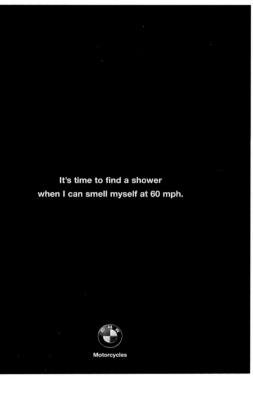

It's time to find a shower
when I can smell myself at 60 mph.

BMW
Motorcycles

orgy of gross drunken behavior.

Because here and there in our men's magazines, sprouting from the dark recesses of marshmallow cleavage and oiled buttocks, are little weeds of contradiction. One of my recent favorites was the sudden profusion of facial and chest hair on male models in fashion shoots. It was as if, having finally woken up to the fact that, generally speaking, gay men no longer sport mustaches, the straight magazines decided to try and reclaim them. Alas, their efforts were undone by Adrian Clark, fashion director of the gay men's magazine *Attitude*, who declared that the new fashion for facial hair was merely a reaction to the increasingly effeminate fashions for men.

"Men's fashion has become camper in the past two seasons," said Clark. "With a beard, I feel I can wear a 'poofy' shirt, like Gucci's shocking pink one, and still look masculine," he told the *Independent*, adding, "My beard gives me more scope and individuality." We must leave aside the likelihood that Clark was sending the paper up—the word *beard* is gay slang for a female companion adopted in order to conceal one's homosexuality, and there is a delightful perversity in the idea of a gay man wearing a beard in order to offset his "poofy" fashions, especially if by announcing this he makes it taboo for a straight man to attempt the same look, in case—horror!—he might be mistaken for a "poof" himself.

The fear of being taken for a "poof" still haunts British masculinity, gliding like a ghost, invisible but somehow palpable, through the pages of our men's magazines. However, times have changed since the early Nineties, when an article of mine for *Arena*, featuring an interview with an openly gay fashion designer, was cut to remove any reference to his sexual preferences.

Then again, this was before pouting seventeen-year-olds in g-strings became standard cover material for most men's magazines, thus providing the straight male consumer with his own "beard"—he can't be queer if he was buying a magazine with a sexy, half-dressed girl on the cover, could he?

If there has been one beneficial aspect of the move towards soft-core, it is the fact that it has allowed space for homosexuality to be tacitly acknowledged, if not fully accepted. As I write, this month's *Arena* features an interview with a camp TV presenter generally thought to be gay, and broaches the matter of his sexuality in an unusually direct way. His answer? "It's nobody's business. . . . I don't actually mind if people think I sleep with women, or if they think I sleep with men. The truth of the matter is that I'm not sleeping with anybody and more's the fucking pity. That is the truth. I'm so up for a shag I cannot tell you." Doubtless this laddish but ultimately evasive answer will have endeared him to the *Arena* readership.

Buffalo Boy,
1988 advertising
campaign for
Pitti Trend.
Photo by
Ray Petri.

175

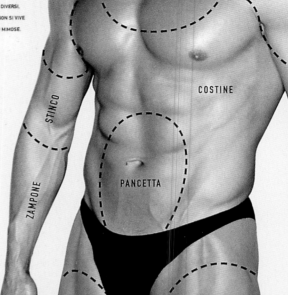

L' 8 MARZO,
DELL'UOMO
NON SI
BUTTA VIA
NIENTE.

SU STUDIO UNIVERSAL.
SONO LE DONNE A FARE
LA FESTA AGLI UOMINI.
SEI FILM PER SEI
UOMINI DIVERSI.
PERCHÉ NON SI VIVE
DI SOLO MIMOSE.

The quest for totems of heterosexual masculinity in a post-homoerotic British media is painfully evident. At the cosier end of the scale is the self-explanatory TV sitcom *Men Behaving Badly*, inspired (if that is the word) by *Loaded*, and stuffed full of jokes about drunkenness, football, and men's untidiness. For those seeking a more aggressive articulation of their gender, there are books. Not just any old books, of course, but "true life" books, written by ex-drug dealers, gangsters, and prizefighters. The nonfiction best-seller lists currently feature two classic examples of the genre, *The Guv'nor* by Lenny McLean and Peter Gerrard, and *Pretty Boy*, by Roy Shaw. McLean was an underworld "enforcer" noted for his ferocity, while for the best part of two decades Shaw was Britain's undisputed bare-knuckle prizefighter. Both books appeal to those eager to celebrate a fast-vanishing world of macho values, inhabited by monosyllabic "real men"—a simpler, less complex world with more sharply defined gender roles. These books, despite their supposed nonconformist themes, essentially hark back to the mythical "good old days" when men were men, and took nonsense from nobody—especially women and queers.

This discourse of disappearing masculinity, which we might call Paradigm Lost, recurs frequently in contemporary British male fiction, too. It first came to attention with the publication of Nick Hornby's phenomenal best-seller *Fever Pitch* in 1992. A novelized version of Hornby's youth, the book revolves around a young man's relationship with an absent father, which is facilitated by their mutual passion for football. Indeed, their only real contact comes on match days, when they go to watch the London club Arsenal together. As Mark Simpson has already noted in his gay reading of Hornby's novel in *Male Impersonators: Men Performing Masculinity*, "A man's love for football is a love of and for manhood, composed of a condensation of introjected (turned inwards) homoerotic desire. Boys discover that football places them in a masculine universe where they can enjoy the company of men and the spectacle of their bodies—as long as it is framed within competition, the struggle for dominance."

This yearning for intimacy and bonding, and its accompanying neurotic search for fixed values, has perhaps shifted focus recently. But if anything, the sense of alienation is even more abject, more urgent than when Hornby stormed the British literary scene eight years ago. The most recent manifestation of Paradigm Lost is the new novel from Britain's best-known and highest-paid newspaper columnist, Tony Parsons, who for many years wrote about male issues for *Arena*. His book *Man and Boy* revolves around the image of Parson's real-life father as the archetype of lost masculinity. A newspaper interview at the time of the book's publication noted that "Parsons needs little prompting to talk about the strength and gentleness of

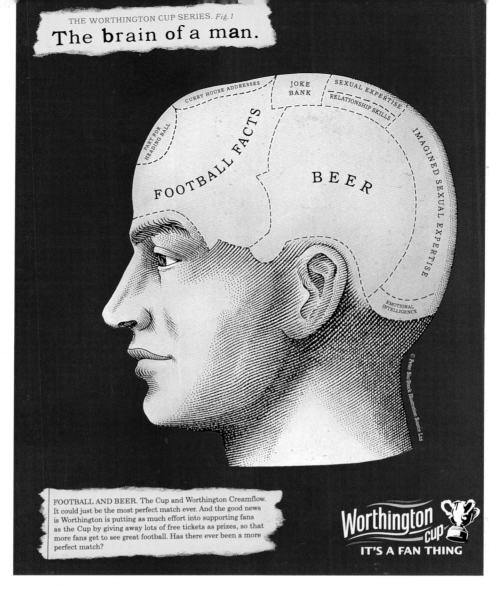

THE WORTHINGTON CUP SERIES. *Fig.1*

The brain of a man.

CURRY HOUSE ADDRESSES · JOKE BANK · SEXUAL EXPERTISE · RELATIONSHIP SKILLS · IMAGINED SEXUAL EXPERTISE · PART FOR HEADING BALL · FOOTBALL FACTS · BEER · EMOTIONAL INTELLIGENCE

© Peter Siu/Stock Illustration Source Ltd

FOOTBALL AND BEER. The Cup and Worthington Creamflow. It could just be the most perfect match ever. And the good news is Worthington is putting as much effort into supporting fans as the Cup by giving away lots of free tickets as prizes, so that more fans get to see great football. Has there ever been a more perfect match?

Worthington cup
IT'S A FAN THING

Advertising campaign for Worthington Cup

facing page: Uomo? Moschino Parfum. Photo by Michelangelo Di Battista

"On March 8, the Festival of Women, we make good use of the whole man," Studio Universal, advertising campaign, 8 March 1999

his father, a wartime commando who became a greengrocer . . . the fictional version is able to overpower two young burglars and tie them up. 'A Freudian would say that [scene] cut to the heart of the way I felt about my father as the Great Protector, and my inability to measure up to him because I could never do a thing like that in a thousand years,' Tony told me. Would the psychiatrist be right? 'God, yeah.'"

At the other end of the scale is one of the country's most successful soccer players, David Beckham. A lean, boyishly handsome man with tastefully highlighted blond hair, Beckham might easily have made a decent living as a male model. This summer he married pop singer Victoria "Posh Spice" Adams in an extravagant wedding ceremony, the picture rights to which were sold to *OK!* for $1.6 million. Beckham was photographed at the wedding reception in a bright purple suit that perfectly matched the color of his bride's floor-length evening gown. (It is interesting to note that Beckham has recently grown a beard.)

Last summer Beckham was vilified as the player who cost England the World Cup, having been sent off for kicking an Argentinian in a quarter-final match that England went on to lose. In fact the kick could hardly be described as that: if anything, Beckham was sent off for sheer petulance.

However, there was already a vast latent well of animosity towards David Beckham among non-United

supporters, stemming from his refusal to revert back to the Paradigm. Instead, he presents a fascinating composite of new and traditional values. During his courtship of Adams, he was photographed on a holiday wearing a sarong. The fact that he was with his fiancée at the time was barely enough to restrain the muted homophobic comments of the tabloid press. Nor has fatherhood modified the popular perception of Beckham as less than an ideal image of masculinity—perhaps because it is he who is most often photographed in public holding the couple's baby son, Brooklyn. This vilification of a hardworking, talented, and wildly successful sportsman—simply because he does not conform to an outdated model of manhood—speaks volumes about the crisis facing British masculinity.

Ironically, this struggle to define contemporary manhood, largely played out in the pages of our men's magazines, is underwritten by men's cosmetics and beauty products. For all its editorializing about boxing, football, and other so-called male pastimes, the men's magazine industry largely owes its expansion to the huge growth in sales of "men's grooming products"—hair gel, foundation creams, lip balm, aftershave, and cologne—which, according to recent figures from Colipa, the European cosmetics industry association, is the new boom area for cosmetics products. Sales of men's toiletries have increased by over 25 per cent in the last five years, with the annual European market net worth nearly $1 billion.

It is this new trend for male beauty products and its attendant homoerotic advertising imagery—"the packaging of a queer lifestyle," as Mark Simpson would have it—that is being offset by the quest for Paradigm Lost, the vain attempt to grasp the last charred shreds of macho certainty from this bonfire of the vanities.

The signs are ominous for British men. It seems that they will live longer, more luxurious, but infinitely less fulfilling lives than their fathers and grandfathers. According to the Continuous Mortality Bureau of the Faculty and Institute of Actuaries, male life expectancy has leaped five years in the last two decades. The average thirty-five-year-old can now expect to live to eighty-five years and one month, whereas in 1980, the life expectancy for a man of the same age was eighty years and one month. The most significant factors, say the institute, are better health care, recent medical advances, and a drastic reduction in smoking.

Yet essentially, despite the vanity and posturing, it seems that young men are unhappy. The fact of increased male longevity masks another, more telling statistic. Government figures show that three times as many British men commit suicide as women. Young men seem particularly prone to self-loathing and despair—among 15-24 year olds, suicide figures have doubled in the last decade, and in this age group suicide is now the second most common cause of death, after traffic accidents. And the number is still rising: just over

a year ago, the government launched a help-line telephone service targeted at young men, in an effort to stop the increasing numbers of young men who kill themselves.

Perhaps they sense the uncertainty of the times. Maybe they realize that—statistically, at least—they are doomed to end their days alone and unloved. According to British market analyst Mintel, in a new report called *Men Living Alone*, a surplus of men in the next two decades will mean that many males will be bachelors by necessity, rather than choice. In 1996 there was a surplus of 230,000 women in the 30-39 age range. By 2007, men will outnumber women for the first time this century in Britain, with an excess of nearly 600,000 men in their mid- to late thirties. Quite simply, many men will find themselves sitting at home alone, wishing they had a partner.

Perhaps then we will see the rise of a new paradigm of rugged individualism to replace the old myths of prizefighters and gangsters. New Men, living on their own. Rugged individualists, doomed to a life of microwaved individual ready meals, their bathroom cabinets overflowing with grooming products, and a stack of glossy men's magazines at their bedsides, the pages dripping with photos of beautiful young women wearing tiny bikinis.

Armand Basi,
spring/summer
1999 advertising
campaign.
Photo by
Garth Meyer

facing page:
advertising
campaign for
Ford Cougar,
1998/99, with
Dennis Hopper

Peppino Ortoleva, Maria Teresa Di Marco

THE FUTURE ADAM

Male Archetypes and Science Fiction

The Future of the Past

The science fiction of the Sixties and the early Seventies—whether it takes the form of film, literature, television, or comic books—is a particularly interesting vantage point from which to observe many of the changes of attitude that have swept the final third of this century. In particular, it offers a remarkable view of emerging gender identities and shifts in our perceptions of masculinity. When we look back to explore how the imagination of the period portrayed man in the year 2000, in the twofold sense (which was not as offensive back then as it is now) of human being and male, we see not only an interesting and somewhat forgotten moment of cultural transition, but also a spectrum of visions of the future that have helped to make us what we are today.

By the Sixties, the fantastic portrayal of the future of humanity in science fiction was not limited to, nor even particularly focused on, the development of technology, the original obsession of the "scientifiction" invented by Hugo Gernsback (the author and scientific popularizer who is generally credited with the introduction of the new genre immediately following the First World War); instead, there was evidenced a broad interest in social structure and change. The exploration of distant worlds had lost many of its more adventuresome connotations and took on—if anything—the aura of so many new examples of Gulliver's travels—explorations of planets or other unknown places

became opportunities to project possible configurations of the future, such as the extreme joke played by Robert Sheckley in his novel *Journey Beyond Tomorrow* (1967), which tells the story of a voyage of initiation and anthropological discovery undertaken by a Polynesian to an advanced space civilization. This Rashomon-style reconstruction confronts the reader with a kaleidoscope of viewpoints on the present and the future, on civilization and what passes for barbarism. Many novels of the period also appear to the eyes of the present-day reader as genuine wagers on the worlds of the future, worlds distinguished not so much by radical innovations in technology as much as by the effects of existing modern technologies taken to their extreme but logical conclusions, worlds of the future imagined chiefly from the point of view of careful, and sometime presumptuous, observations of the world of the present.

The characters, female and especially male (at the time, as has been demonstrated by Darko Suvin—generally considered the leading sociologist and scholar of the genre—science fiction was enjoyed primarily by males, not unlike video games at their debut), appear far less "alien" than many protagonists of the science fiction of the previous period, between the Thirties and the Fifties, with its obsession with outer space and machinery. They were more like caricatures of ordinary everyday people, as could be expected from a genre that often verged on the satirical, but caricatures in the etymological sense of the word as well: "charged," with a peculiar and, even today, seductive energy.

This may be the reason why the hyper-simplified outfits, almost Chinese in their austerity, worn by Marcello Mastroianni in Elio Petri's *The Tenth Victim* (1965), the uniforms of the firemen/pyromaniacs of François Truffaut's *Fahrenheit 451* (1966), or the strange fashion and ultra-materialist habits of the *Space Merchants* (1962), a novel by Frederik Pohl and C.M. Kornbluth (1962), are so deeply impressed in our collective memory.

The same could not be said of the characters of the admittedly fascinating literary visions of the future of the fin de siècle, with the possible exception of the disturbing *L'Eve Future* (1886) by Count Auguste Villiers de l'Isle-Adam, which has rightly enough been recently rediscovered. And we have nothing but scorn for the stylized little figurines of the science fiction of the Thirties or the early Fifties, with their obsessively aerodynamic lines and their futuristic conformism, that fell target to the corrosive irony of William Gibson in his short story "The Gernsback Continuum" (1986): "They were blond. They were standing beside their car, an aluminum avocado with a central shark-fin rudder jutting up from its spine and smooth black tires like a child's toy. . . . They were both in white: loose clothing, bare legs, spotless white sun shoes. . . . They were Heirs to the Dream. . . . They were white, blond, and they probably had blue eyes." And they were similar, in an unsettling manner, to the Nazi fantasies

of an Aryan humanity of the future. The styles that were prevalent in the science fiction of those years of the Cold War appear today, again to borrow phrases from William Gibson, no less distant than so many odd and damaged archeological finds: "An architecture of broken dreams . . . Coca-Cola plants like beached submarines, and fifth-run movie houses like the temples of some lost sect that had worshipped blue mirrors and geometry."

These were the styles made popular as well by Fred M. Wilcox's *Forbidden Planet* (1956), a film that exerted considerable influence, especially in Great Britain. It is said that Mary Quant was particularly swayed by it.

On the other hand, the future images of people, customs, and clothing that appeared in the Sixties are still with us: the sect that adored them has not vanished; rather, it might be, indeed probably is, one of the many sects that make up the New Age galaxy. This cannot be explained alone by the longevity of television series such as

The Avengers

facing page:
Keir Dullea in
2001: A Space Odyssey, 1968,
directed by
Stanley Kubrick

Star Trek, itself a significant factor. The vitality of those images derives, on the one hand, from their presentation, even today, as directional signals, indications of what we shall become, and, on the other hand, by their peculiar and specific ambiguity.

Directional Signals

Forbidden Planet with Leslie Nielsen and Anne Francis, 1956, directed by Fred M. Wilcox

The Sixties was the decade during which we became aware that there was an irreversible crisis in the very idea of progress, a time when an alternative idea began to appear and sink roots in the common viewpoint (as is demonstrated by the sudden and immense popularity of Marshall McLuhan between 1964 and 1970), a belief that the future is not something that needs to be constructed but rather that the future is already here; it is just that we haven't really noticed, and we need to become aware of it. Science fiction, but also the nascent field of semiology, invited us all to find evidence of this present/future in everyday life, especially in the appearance—anything but "superficial"—of persons and objects, thus reinforcing a phenomenon that was in time to alter radically the social perception of apparel: a refined obsession with styles.

An Ambiguous Future

The future portrayed in the science fiction of the Sixties was ambiguous in ideological terms because utopia appeared in science fiction as no longer separate from and opposed to dystopia, or the negative utopia, as it had been in the Fifties; instead the two were powerfully and indissolubly intertwined. We need only think of Stanley Kubrick's film *2001: A Space Odyssey* (1968), which was at once a celebration of and death knell for the old science fiction: here, the delights of interstellar space travel are brusquely interrupted, though not eliminated, by the obscure episode of the deranged and despotic supercomputer HAL, a full-fledged nightmare of a coming future. And it is ambiguous in terms of taste, because science fiction, like all genres directed at even a moderately cultivated audience, was swept in those years by the triumph of camp, a perceptual and esthetic transformation that has yet to run out of influence. Camp has its obsessive fascination with irony and therefore with the double and triple significance of every object and every narrative. It is ambiguous, as well, in terms of gender.

Gender and Sex

It is precisely for the barely concealed ambiguity of gender identity that the science fiction of the period seems so close to us; indeed, we should refer to a full-fledged obsession with the theme, which, especially in the comic versions, took on some very odd forms, including a mania for the question of the sex of aliens, no less surreal in the final analysis than the earlier preoccupation with the sex of angels. Among the reasons for the phenomenon is surely the liberalization of personal habits and customs; the progressive but extremely rapid disappearance of taboos in the mass media, and especially in film; and the gradual lowering of the barriers of obscenity that took place at the time, and that was surprisingly easy and peaceful

(but certainly not without social and psychological consequences). Among the "canonic" genres of mass culture, science fiction was one of the first to relax its censorship. This was surely due in part to the characteristics of its audience, urban and relatively well educated, but also perhaps to more intrinsic factors. The fall of erotic taboos, especially the first phase prior to its absolute wholesale banalization, was, in fact, easily, almost naturally, projected into the future, in a utopia of universal liberation or else a dystopia of biblical dimensions, a Sodom on the horizon.

Nowadays, accustomed as we are to widespread obscenity and the many and varied perverse looks of fashion, it is difficult to remember the diffuse aura of surprise and fascination that surrounded the first, tentative liberalization of pornography, as well as the complexity and ambiguity of that transition, in terms of values. The "cultural" message that accompanied the collapse of the barriers of censorship pushed toward a collapse of all traditional phallocentric restrictions and, at the same time—though there was, at least initially, no understanding of the intrinsic conflicts this would create—toward the satisfaction of all erotic desires, including those most deeply rooted in centuries of authoritarian and aggressive masculine imagination.

Barbarella (the star of the comic book launched by Jean-Claude Forest in 1962 and the heroine played by Jane Fonda in the movie by Roger Vadim in 1968) coexisted for a number of years with liberationist utopias, until the first feminists denounced the contradictions that were intrinsic to this coexistence.

Perhaps, however, the ambiguity of the depiction of gender so typical of the science fiction of that period was a response to something deeper than the sudden collapse of the walls of censorship—admittedly important, and still only partially understood—and even deeper than the still-less-well-understood effects of the birth control pill and the sudden separation of sexuality and procreation. What was

at play here was a twofold portrayal of the future of man: on the one hand, a vision that projected the entire future of humanity into an ascetic unisex world that was actually a generalized, neutralized maleness made "universal"; on the other, a vision that was just beginning to grasp the idea that maleness was a gender, distinct and endowed with its own characteristics. In our effort to understand this latter transition, the science fiction of this period is a litmus test.

Masculine, Feminine; Neuter?

Let's take a step backward. As long as can be remembered, the term *man,* itself a designation of a gender, summarized and represented humanity at large; to say "man" is the same as saying "humanity." For that matter, while the female body was historically a written and eloquent body, in which the symbolic element emerged beyond—and paradoxically through—the material aspects of gender, the male body represented the neutral body, the human body that needs no definition, which simply is. It is no accident, for instance, that in the anatomical depiction of the body in the nineteenth-century wax figurines by Susini preserved in the Museo della Specola in Florence, the male body is simply nude, while the female body is dressed, adorned, and posed, to the point of being flirtatious, despite possessing arteries and viscera open to view. The association, taken for granted, of human and male, left women in the past with an overwhelming problem of how to define themselves, even though the woman's body was eloquent (largely because it was a body written by men).

When, however, the very meaning of the term *human* was laid open to question by technical, scientific, and social changes in the Sixties, what appeared immediately to become unstable was the historically determined identity of the male. It is clear that masculinity, like femininity—but perhaps to an even greater degree—is not merely a biological question. The demise, or at any rate, the reconfiguration of models of masculinity based wholly on physical strength was unquestionably linked, on the one hand, to the emancipation of female roles and awareness, but on the other hand, and this should not be overlooked, to the growing awareness that many traditionally male jobs would be replaced by machinery. Certainly, in one sense technological advances per se were tantamount to forms of emancipation for men and for women. For women, however, technological advances, be they electric home appliances or birth control pills, were perceived, rightly or wrongly, as entirely liberating; for men, there was a growing problem of a sense of obsolescence, of being replaced in practical and theoretical terms. It is no accident that one of the most evident and immediate repercussions of this transition can be found in the narrative genre that most directly focuses upon technology and the world that technology creates: science fiction.

Look again at the image of the supercomputer with a male voice, HAL, as it expels from the spaceship, and

Jane Fonda and John Phillip Law in *Barbarella*, 1968, directed by Roger Vadim

facing page: *Fahrenheit 451*, 1966, with Oskar Werner and Julie Christie, directed by François Truffaut

185

therefore from human and terrestrial space, an astronaut, who drifts off like so much stellar garbage into the absolute void of the cosmos. This sets the tone for an entire wave of masculine anguish regarding the near future. It presents a crisis not only in the prerogatives linked to physical strength, but also in the value of technical know-how and skill: for those who establish their identity on the things they are able to do (taking for granted the naturalness and centrality of their own being), it promises a collapse of the most basic certainties of identity.

Overwhelmed, then, by radical changes in the social sphere, but even more important, in the technical and scientific sphere, man finds himself faced for the first time with the problem of defining himself, his role, and his proper mental disposition. Under the circumstances, it is quite natural to encounter the opposite extremes of the macho, on the one hand, and the androgyne, on the other, which—it is no coincidence—mirrors perfectly the stereotypical female opposition between virgin and whore. This new need to write a male body, much as we have always written a female body, is reflected in fashion through the plasticity of models, all of which have become equally possible, since there no longer exists an ontological definition of the male.

The Sixties Again: A Chinese Look

The depiction of the masculine—and here, too, science fiction in the Sixties was well ahead of its time—is largely and primarily based on outfit and look. Indeed, and this is very significant, the outfit that remains impressed in our memory from Sixties science fiction is primarily masculine, whether it be a uniform or civilian dress. Women's clothing was almost always a caricature, the expression of a recurring campy irony, from the funny space stewardesses in Kubrick's film to the Barbarella of film and funnies, all with outfits that might well have been made of some imaginary futuristic material but that were always and especially dotted with holes and gaps scattered strategically over the body. These garments turned their wearers into objects of appetite more than femmes fatales and were certainly unlikely to inspire styles or trigger

trends (even though the outfits worn by Jane Fonda in Vadim's *Barbarella* were designed by Paco Rabanne and were featured in fashion magazines for several months). If it is true, as much magazine and newspaper journalism would seem to suggest, that the historical development of men's clothing describes a line of progressive simplification (in counterpoint to the dynamic cycles of women's wear and fashion, which is of course "female"), then in the science fiction of the Sixties, that evolution reached a sort of terminal point, at once extreme and natural, in the suit devoid of any hem, lapel, or other adornment whatsoever. This image was widely diffused, not only by science fiction but also by rock stars beginning with the Beatles and the Who, and was curiously similar to the Chinese look that, interestingly, was presented at the same time as the natural culmination of the unisex trend and as an application to the field of apparel of that taste for rational design that still seems so distinctively characteristic of the Sixties. In reality, these are two complementary aspects, tending in each case to be not the object of an arbitrary esthetic choice, but the logical and rational consequence of biological and cultural factors.

In the final analysis, however, the spread of the "Chinese" model ought to remind us of another aspect of the culture of the period: the fact that the widespread hatred of uniforms corresponded to an equally widespread need to analyze "as uniforms" the clothing of the everyday, in which one sought out signs of ideological alliance or even shared musical tastes, or even, in the following decade, sexual preferences.

Men's clothing can aspire to suppress any and all capricious and gratuitous variations, which are precisely what fashion requires; men's clothing can offer unmistakable signs of affiliation. There is seemingly an unsolvable contradiction between these two models: on the one hand, blank clothing, a zero degree of expression; on the other, "written" clothing, bearer of signs. In reality, these are two complementary choices, in each case tending to make clothing a dependent variable, not subject to esthetic choice, but the consequence of other biological or cultural factors, and thus apparently more "rational" than clothing subject to the apparent caprices of fashion and taste. It was this supposed rationality that was proffered, for a certain period successfully, to women as well as men, in the declared intention of freeing them from the uncertain patterns and the subordinate gender roles that were long considered intrinsic to the very idea of fashion.

The Seventies and Eighties: Dangerous Games

Subsequently, however, in the Seventies and the early Eighties, the ambiguity in the perception of gender, body, and sex took deeper root and lost much of the lucid playfulness of the preceding decade; or perhaps we should say, identity was transformed into a game, but a dangerous one. And, once again, it is science fiction that explains it to us before other genres, in the words, for instance, of James Ballard, in his preface to the French edition of *Crash* (1974): "[The] loss of emotional faculties has opened the way to all of our most concrete and delicate pleasures, those of the delights of pain and mutilation, of sex as a perfect forum, as a substrate or culture in which to breed sterile pus, for all of the most exquisite bullfighters' veronicas of our perversions, of the moral freedom to attend to our psychopathology as if it were a game."

In this new context, masculinity, in science fiction and elsewhere, has undergone new pressures and new deformations, in terms of clothing and in terms of the portrayal of identity: it splits between its "universalist" variant, which leans toward "androgyny," and a more specific and idiosyncratic version that offers a hyper-masculine, aggressive (and often subtly ironic) exaltation of virility that takes the direct depiction of the phallus as its most authentic symbol. It is the masculinity of George Miller's *Mad Max* (1979) and James Cameron's *Terminator* (1984), with its unsettling competition between the machine/body of Arnold Schwarzenegger and the "I am strong and sexy" message implied in the image of Linda Hamilton.

At the same time, the variability of forms and styles has gradually extended in direct proportion to the disappearance of meaning: if, in the uniform/outfit, whether military or not, individual details had always conveyed profound consequences in symbolic terms, now the variability takes the form of a game played on the surface, with which one enters the circular and frivolous world of feminine fashion. The classic style, in this context, is nothing more than a form among forms, and certainly no longer the form, since there is no longer a man/human capable of embodying it.

The Nineties: Prosthetic Extensions of Identity

Still later, but in continuity with the same process, science fiction of the Nineties proffers the image of male bodies "rehabilitated" by a technological surplus; it is as if that which had so profoundly given rise to the crisis of masculine identity were now being reinterpreted in terms of a new enhancement. In this connection, the psychoanalyst Darian Leader, in *Why Do Women Write More Letters Than They Send?* (1997), points out that the transmission of "virile values" today no longer takes place on a symbolic level. An effort is therefore made to compensate for this incapacity to be and to become men in the traditional sense by seeking out technological cure-alls capable of adding something more to the simple biological fact, which alone is insufficient.

These prosthetic extensions of identity must be grafted directly onto the corporeal tissue in that blend of man and machine that is often depicted as one of the

most specific characters of contemporary culture. We still must wonder whether, as Leader believes, technological grafting specifically affects masculinity, or whether, on the contrary, it expresses the very ambiguity of gender. In effect, the characteristics of this new "virility" are connoted traditionally in terms of strength and power, but they do not actually call into question the old issues of identity. As in a sort of video game, it is possible to gather from the ground a number of weapons, a number of special powers, that offer temporary and changing identities, without allowing those identities to acquire any real and lasting value. Power, which is still a virile attribute (but no longer necessarily male), is capable by virtue of a technological surplus of offering a transitory masculinity, but that is only one of the many noncontradictory forms of a new identity. In this direction lies the concept of transgender, which deeply permeates the new cyber-feminist literature: it proclaims the cyborg organism, a blend of human and technological, as a way to overcome even the reality of opposing identities—black versus white, male versus female, man versus machine.

The future is held out, then, as a place of fluid identities, where being male and being female is strictly a matter of external attributes: identity is no longer determined by gender, but is assumed through the appropriation of roles. If we are to indicate the direction in which the Future Adam is evolving, it no longer seems possible to reason in terms of a single and unified definition, nor in terms of a broad and all-encompassing definition of masculinity. An omnium-gatherum of variable attributes "freely" chosen, masculinity finds itself moving ever closer to the exquisitely feminine paradox of just having no idea what to wear.

Mel Gibson in *Mad Max Beyond Thunderdome*, 1985, directed by George Miller and George Ogilvie

facing page: The Vulcan Spock, played by Leonard Nimoy in the television series *Star Trek*, created by Gene Roddenberry

187

Photographs by Roberta Orio

ADAM'S APPLE

*Kult, Codice
Umano*, 1994-97.
Photos by
Roberta Orio

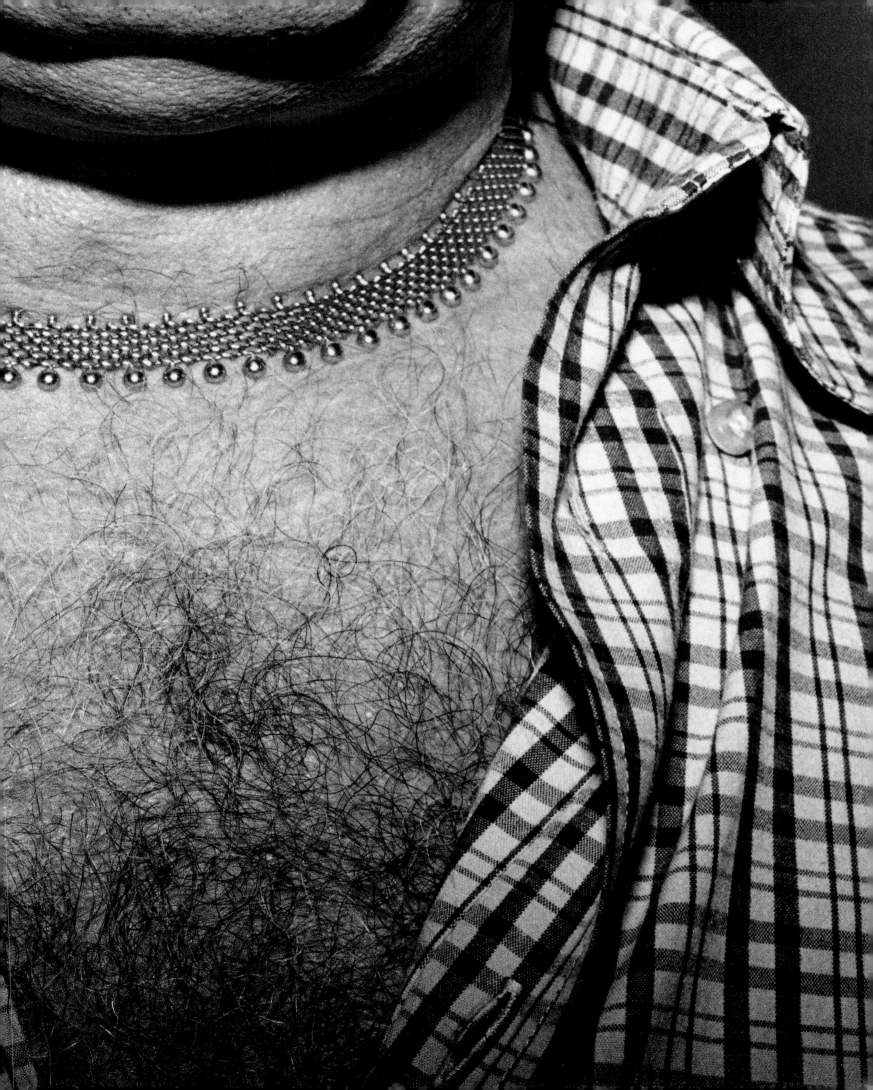

BIOGRAPHIES

Carlo Antonelli

Carlo Antonelli, producer for the recording label Sugar, is a writer and a music critic. He is the co-author, with Fabio De Luca, of a book of essays, *Discoinferno. Storia della Dance Italiana dalla Preistoria ad Oggi* (Rome, 1995), and of *Fuori Tutti. Una Generazione in Camera Sua* (Turin, 1996, with photographs by Marco Delogu). In the years 1997-1998 he conceived and co-wrote, with Lilli Forina, a television series called "Raieducational Infinito Futuro." He regularly teaches seminars on the esthetics of music at the Istituto Europeo di Design, in Milan.

Natalia Aspesi

This leading Italian journalist lives and works in Milan. She writes for the Italian newspaper *La Repubblica*, and has done so since the first issue.

Andrea Balestri

Andrea Balestri is an economist; since 1988 he has been the director of the Research Center of the Association of Manufacturers of Prato; since 1993 he has directed that association's Group for Communications and Promotion. He teaches at various universities and schools (including the University of Florence, Libero Istituto Universitario Carlo Cattaneo in Castellanza, Bocconi University in Milan, and Hosey University in Tokyo). He is a member of the secretariat of the Club dei Distretti Industriali. He edits two periodical publications (the monthly *Pratofutura* and the quarterly *Distretti Italiani*), and has published extensively in such publications as *Scienze ed Esperienze, La Laniera, Mondo Economico, La Nazione, Il Sole 24 Ore, L'Impresa, Sviluppo Locale, Economia e Management*, and *L'Illustrazione Italiana*.

Carlo Bertelli

Carlo Bertelli is currently an Emeritus Professor at the University of Lausanne and professor of the history of ancient art at the Academy of Architecture in Mendrisio (University of Italian Switzerland). He has served as the Commissioner for Historic Heritage in Milan and was the Director of the Pinacoteca di Brera. He has taught in various universities in Italy (Venice, Milan) and around the world (aside from Lausanne, Geneva, Berkeley, and Berlin). As a member of the board of the XVI Triennale (1978-1981) he was the first to introduce the topic of fashion into the temple of architecture and design. He is the author of numerous books and essays, and has focused on aspects of dress and costume in works of art. In 1999 he delivered the Mellon Lectures at the National Gallery of Art in Washington, D.C. He is currently working on an exhibition entitled *The Future of the Longobards*, which will be held in Brescia in 2001.

Uta Brandes

With degrees in sociology and psychology, Uta Brandes did her post-graduate work at the University of Hannover, where she later worked as a professor and as the deputy director of a research institute working on women's issues. She founded the Center for Swiss Design in Langenthal and she directed the Forum of the Art Fair of the German Federal Republic in Bonn. Among the various books she has published are monographic works on Dieter Rams, frogdesign, Ralf Fehlbaum, Richard Sapper, F. A. Porsche, and Kurt Weidemann; she has also edited a series of books on the "future of the senses."

Thomas Hine

Thomas Hine writes about design, mass culture, and architecture. He is the author of *Populuxe*, an analysis of the look and life of America in the Fifties and Sixties, which also gave the English language a new word to define the style of that period. His most recent book is *The Rise and Fall of the American Teenager* (New York, 1999).

Franco La Cecla

Franco La Cecla is a researcher in the department of literature at the University of Bologna; he teaches the sociology of interethnic relations in the department of literature at the University of Palermo and cultural anthropology in the department of cultural preservation at the University of Ravenna. He is the author of *Perdersi, l'Uomo Senza Ambiente* (Bari, 1988); *Mente Locale, per un'Antropologia dell'Abitare* (Rome, 1993); *Il Malinteso, Antropologia dell'Incontro* (Bari, 1997), and various other publications. Among these are *Bambini per strada* (Milan, 1995) and *Perfetti e Invisibili. L'Immagine dell'Infanzia nei Media* (Milan, 1996), the latter resulting in an exhibition as well, which he curated for Pitti Immagine in Florence in 1995.

David Le Breton

David Le Breton is a professor of anthropology in the department of social sciences at the University of Strasbourg II. He is the author of *Les Passions ordinaires. Anthropologie des Emotions, Du Silence*, and *L'Adieu au Corps*.

Mark Lipson

Mark Lipson studied at the University of Toronto and at the School of Film and Television at New York University. His first interest is photography, but he has also shot various feature-length films, among them *The Thin Blue Line*. He has taken part in numerous collective shows, and he has done photographic shoots for various magazines, including *Vanity Fair* and *Raygun*. In 1998 he held a monographic show of the work he has done over the past twenty years with the Polaroid SX-70. His photographs of Lucha Libre form part of a body of work focusing on the relationships between body and culture.

Anna Lombardi

Anna Lombardi, industrial designer (I.S.I.A., Rome 1979), worked as an assistant to Alessandro Mendini and, from 1983 to 1986, as a member for cultural planning of the IDZ (International Design Zentrum) of Berlin, in the group directed by F. Burkhardt. She was a founding member SAD, Società Artisti e Designers, which—operating from 1985 to 1988—was one of the first groups of designers producing their own products in Italy; she has also worked with Alessi, Moroso, Giancarlo Giannini SpA, Metallurgica Lux, and Fantoni. She curated the design section in the exhibitions *Nuove Contaminazioni* (1996), *Design: Progetto Formazione* (1998), and *Cent'Anni di Sedie* (1999) for the Galleria d'Arte Moderna in Udine.

Peppino Ortoleva

Peppino Ortoleva is the author of about a hundred publications, including essays and books on the history and theory of communications. Among his recent books are *Mediastoria. Comunicazione e Mutamento Sociale nel Mondo Contemporaneo* (Parma, 1995) and *Un Ventennio a Colori. Televisione Privata e Società in Italia* (Florence, 1995). He teaches theory and techniques of the new media in the department of communications sciences at the University of Turin and is a part-owner of Cliomedia, a company that works in the fields of multimedia production, mass communications, and historic and social research.

Ted Polhemus

Ted Polhemus is an anthropologist who has specialized since the Seventies in the relations between youth cultures and fashion. Among his various publications are *Fashion-Antifashion* (1975) and *Street Style, from Sidewalk to Catwalk* (1994), published in conjunction with the exhibition of the same name at the Victoria and Albert Museum in London.

Marco Ricchetti

Marco Ricchetti is an economist and the director of the Department of Economic Research of Federtessile, the association of textiles manufacturers, where he is also adviser to the chairman. He has written about economic and financial cycles in the textiles industry, and he is also Federtessile's director of research for commercial policy initiatives on national and European levels.

Giannino Malossi

Giannino Malossi is an author and media consultant; from the Seventies on, he has played a role in the theoretical and practical development of a "culture of fashion" in Italy. He has undertaken numerous research projects that resulted in his curating exhibitions (*Il Senso della Moda*, XIV Triennale of Milan, 1979; *Tipologie dei Comportamenti di Moda*, Venice Biennale—Progetti Speciali, 1980; *Ricerca sul Decoro*, Centro Domus, Milan 1981) and has authored various publications, among them *Liberi tutti, Vent'Anni di Moda Spettacolo* (Milan, 1987); *Apparel Art—Fashion Is the News* (Milan, 1989); *This Was Tomorrow. Pop Design da Stile a Revival* (Milan, 1990); *La Sala Bianca, Nascita della Moda Italiana* (Milan, 1992); *La Regola Estrosa, Cent'Anni di Eleganza Italiana* (Milan, 1993); *Latin Lover, The Passionate South* (Milan, 1996); *The Style Engine* (New York, 1998); and *Volare—The Icon of Italy in Global Pop Culture* (New York, 1999).

Claudio Risé

Claudio Risé is a psychoanalyst, considered by some to be the "leading Italian specialist in masculinity." For many years he worked as a journalist for *L'Espresso*; he is now a professor at the University of Trieste and he writes a regular column for Io Donna. He has written a book entitled *Il Maschio Selvatico* and numerous other works on psychology.

Roberta Orio

Roberta Orio has worked as a photographer since studying under Roberto Salbitani. Since 1989 she has held numerous shows and published many books. In 1998 she began teaching a course in industrial design in the department of architecture at the University of Milan. In 1999 she won the national award Chimica Aperta. She specializes in social photography and landscape, art, and monumental photography; she also pursues artistic photography.

Roberto Schezen

Roberto Schezen held shows of his work in the Eighties in Galleria Il Diaframma in Milan and Galleria Rondanini in Rome. In 1987 he held a personal show at the Cooper Union in New York, entitled *Places and Memories*. His most recent exhibition, *Epic Forms*, which included pictures shown in this book, was held at the Edwynn Houk Gallery in New York in 1998. Since the late Seventies, Schezen has published many books with various publishers, including Rizzoli International, The Monacelli Press, and Harry N. Abrams, Inc.

Alix Sharkey

Alix Sharkey began writing in 1981, working for the taboo-breaking magazine *i-D*. He has written extensively over the years on nightlife, fashion, the media, advertising, and youth culture, for such publications as *The Guardian, The Independent, The Sunday Times*, and *The Observer*. He also was the news director for MTV Europe from 1992 to 1993. He writes for various European and American publications, including *Dazed & Confused, Condé Nast Traveller, Das Magazin* and *Courier International*. He lives in London.

Antony Shugaar

Antony Shugaar is a journalist, translator, and author. He has published three books (for Arcadia, Aguilar, and Smithmark), translated many books (for Farrar, Straus & Giroux, Harvard University Press, Abbeville Press, The MIT Press, and others), and published numerous articles (*The New York Observer, Spy, New York Magazine, Photo District News, Wigwag, New England Monthly*, and others). He worked on the planning and production of the projects *The Style Engine* and *Volare—The Icon of Italy in Global Pop Culture*. He is especially interested in the media industry and the creation of meaning in pop, popular, and classical cultures.

Valerie Steele

Valerie Steele is chief curator at the museum of the Fashion Institute of Technology, where she taught for ten years. She is a cultural historian and has written many books; among her most recent titles are *Fifty Years of Fashion. New Look to Now* (New Haven, 1997); *Fetish: Fashion, Sex and Power* (London, 1996). She curated the exhibition *Art, Design and Barbie: The Making of a Cultural Icon*. She edits the quarterly publication *Fashion Theory: The Journal of Dress, Body & Culture*. She is a member of the boards of the Costume Society of America and the International Costume Association (Tokyo), and she is a member of the Fashion Group International.

Stefano Torrione

Stefano Torrione took a degree in political science before pursuing photography as a career. For years, he has been working in the areas of geographic and social journalism, with leading Italian and international publications. In 1994 he was awarded the Kodak Panorama European Prize at Arles (France) for his work on street children in Bucharest.

Ugo Volli

Ugo Volli teaches the philosophy of language at the University of Bologna and semiotics at the University IULM of Milan. He is particularly interested in issues of communications, in both theoretical and practical terms. He has done a great deal of work on fashion, and among his publications in this field are *Contro la Moda* (1988); *Una Scrittura del Corpo* (1998); and Block Modes (1998); he writes for such newspapers and magazines as *La Repubblica, Il Mattino, Grazia*, and *Liberal*. He has published many books; among the most recent ones are *Il Libro della Comunicazione* (1994); *Come Leggere il Telegiornale* (1995); *Fascino* (1997); and *Il Televoto* (1997).

Alain Weill

Alain Weill lives in Paris. He holds a doctorate in jurisprudence and a DEA in semiology and the sociology of art and literature. He is an expert in art, contemporary graphics, and advertising, and has authored about thirty publications on related topics, and in particular on poster art. Since 1990 he has been the director of the International Meetings on Graphic Arts in Chaumont (an annual event, focusing in 1999 on music in posters). He is an official expert on graphics and advertising for Parisian auction houses. He also works for numerous international expositions in Japan, Europe, and the United States and he is the director of the collection of graphic arts of the Bibliothèque Nationale de l'Image. He has presided over or formed part of various international juries for international graphics art awards, including the VGD (Berlin) and the O.B.I. (New York). A noted expert on foods and wines, he is the president of the Conseil National des Arts Culinaires. He writes a weekly food column in the publication *L'Evénement du Jeudi*. In 1997 he published the book *Ma garde-robe*.

We would like to thank the
individuals and organizations
listed here for their kind
assistance:

Armand Basi
Cerruti 1881
Diesel Spa
Dolce & Gabbana Spa
Dries Van Noten
Ermenegildo Zegna Spa
Fiorucci Srl
Gianfranco Ferré Spa
Gianni Versace Spa
Gigli Spa
Giorgio Armani Spa
Gruppo GFT
Gucci Spa
I.P.I. Services Spa
Ittierre Spa
Kookaï
Laura Biagiotti Spa
Moschino MoonShadow Spa
Paul Smith
Salvatore Ferragamo Italia Spa
Valentino Spa
Vivienne Westwood

Alessi Spa
Black & Decker Italia Spa
BMW of North America, Inc.
Capitol Records
Jeep, DaimlerChrysler
Philips Spa
Sony Playstation
Volvo Italia Spa
Warp Records

i-D magazine
Arena Homme Plus

Sean Connery
in *Goldfinger*,
1964, directed
by Guy Hamilton

Photo Credits

Edwynn Houk Gallery, New York pp. 106/113
Galleria Emi Fontana, Milan pp. 25, 127
Tomio Koyama Gallery, Tokyo p. 130

Bozell WorldWide, Detroit p. 171
Columbus BB, Florence pp. 174/175
D'Adda, Lorenzini, Vigorelli, Milan p. 176
Jung Von Matt, Hamburg p. 172
Officina delle invenzioni, Milan pp. 8/9
TBWA, London pp. 4/5
Young & Rubicam Italia, Rome p. 178

Archivio Storico Fiat, Turin p. 132
Baron & Baron, Inc., New York p. 80
Farabolafoto, Milan pp. 28, 30, 35, 69,
91, 95, 101, 104, 105, 124/125, 135,
138, 163, 164, 168, 186, 187
Grazia Neri, Milan pp. 20, 90, 169
Katz Pictures/IPG/Contrasto, Milan p. 85
Magnum Photos/Contrasto, Milan pp. 26,
32/33, 42, 45, 68, 70/71, 86, 88,
131, 134, 137
MovieStore Collection, London pp. 34, 67,
102, 103, 180 182/183, 184, 185, 199
R.E.A./Contrasto, Milan p. 133
Scala, Florence pp. 115, 116/117, 118,
119, 121, 122, 123, 125, 128, 136,
Associated Press Italia, Milan pp. 12/13,
22, 27, 29, 31

*The editor and the publisher have made
every effort to obtain permission to use all
illustrations and images and to credit their
sources properly. Any omissions will be
corrected in future editions.*